Y0-ABG-784

The Day of Doom

**Or, A Poetical Description of The Great
and Last Judgement**

By

Michael Wigglesworth

With an Introduction by
Mark Ludwig

American Eagle Publications, Inc.
Post Office Box 41401
Tucson, Arizona 85717
- 1991 -

PS871
.D3
1966

© 1991 by American Eagle Publications.

Originally printed in 1662 by Samuel Green
in Cambridge, Massachusetts.

This edition based on the fifth edition, published in 1701
by B. Green and J. Allen, Boston, Massachusetts.

Library of Congress Cataloging-in-Publication Data

Wigglesworth, Michael, 1631-1705.
     The day of doom, or, A poetical description of the Great and Last
Judgement / by Michael Wigglesworth ; with an introduction by Mark
Ludwig.
          p.   cm.
     ISBN 0-929408-05-5 : $5.95
     1. Judgement Day—Poetry.   I. Title.   II. Title: Poetical
description of the Great and Last Judgement.
PS871.D3   1991
821'.4—dc20   91-38548
                                                                                    CIP

Contents

Introduction

When first published in 1662, *The Day of Doom* proved to be a phenomenal success. In fact, one could reasonably argue that it was the most popular book ever published in America. The entire first edition—1800 copies—sold out in the first year. While that number may seem small today, one must remember that the population of all of New England was only about 30,000 at the time.[1] At least twelve more editions during the next century established *The Day of Doom* not only as a best-seller, but as an enduring work which gained a respect and authority in the lives of the Puritans perhaps second only to the Bible. Adults relied on it, and many school children memorized it from start to finish.

Cotton Mather went so far as to suggest that *The Day of Doom* might be read until the last day which is its theme.[2] However, during the 19th and 20th centuries, literary critics engaged in such a thorough campaign of revisionism that Wigglesworth was almost buried in obscurity—along with many other colonial writers.

Romantic and modern critics who did not have the same standards for truth, beauty, and style as the Puritans have set the tone for literary criticism of early American literature for nearly two centuries. Rather than accepting Puritan standards, looking upon them as quaint curiosities, or trying to understand their place in history, many critics chose simply to attack the Puritans in an attempt to discredit their values. The resulting negative judgements have, by repetition, gained the force of authority. Michael Wigglesworth has borne the brunt of this attack on Puritan culture and faith.

Typical of the attack on Puritans and on Wigglesworth are Moses Coit Tyler's comments, published in his *History of American Literature* in 1878. In discussing the Puritan he begins in very general terms, looking at the positive aspects of their society, but then focuses matters he obviously considered to be excesses in a society "supressing sweetness

---

1. Franklin B. Dexter, "Estimates of Population in the American Colonies" *Proceedings of the American Antiquarian Society*, **5** (October 1887), p. 26.
2. Cotton Mather, *A Faithful Man, Described and Rewarded*, (Boston: B. Green, 1705).

and gaiety in the human heart."[3] He discusses a host of old-fashioned punishments for various crimes and heresies, in an attempt to lead the reader to symphathize with his conclusion,

> "Doubtless we shall be ready to say with Nathaniel Hawthorne: 'Let us thank God for having given us such ancestors; and let each successive generation thank Him not less fervently for being one step further from them in the march of ages.'"[4]

Next, Tyler turns to the literary accomplishments of the Puritans, of which he writes, "In many ways their literary development was stunted and stiffened by the narrowness of puritanism."[5] After a general discusion, Tyler examines individual writers. To some he is kind, but upon Wigglesworth he heaps only contempt. Introducing him to his readers, he writes,

> "In contemporaneous renown, far above all other verse-writers of the colonial time, was Michael Wigglesworth, the explicit and unshrinking rhymer of the Five Points of Calvinism . . . . No one holding a different theology from that held by Michael Wigglesworth, can do justice to him as a poet, without exercising the utmost intellectual catholicity; otherwise, disgust and detestation for much of this poet's message, will drown all sense of the picturesqueness, the imaginative vigor, the tremendous realism, of many of the conceptions under which his message was delivered."[6]

Of *The Day of Doom* he writes

> "A sensitive, firm, wide-ranging, unresting spirit, he looks out mournfully over the throngs of men that fill the world,—all of them totally depraved, all of them caught, from the farthest eternity, in the adamantine meshes of God's decree; the most of them, also being doomed in advance, by those decrees, to an endless existence of ineffable torment,—and upon this situation of affairs, the excellent Michael Wigglesworth proposes to make poetry . . . . This great poem . . . with entire unconciousness, attributes to the Divine Being a character the most execrable and loathsome to be met with, perhaps, in any literature, Christian or pagan . . . . Happily, his frightful and blasphemous delineation of the government exercized over us by the Good God, has at last, in civilized society, lost its cruel power over the human mind."[7]

Other critics were more or less harsh on Wigglesworth, and some have paid him the ultimate insult of ignoring his work altogether. Such

---

3. Moses Coit Tyler, *A History of American Literature*, 2 vols. (New York: G.P. Putnam's Sons, 1878), I, p. 104.
4. Tyler, I, p. 109.
5. Tyler, I, p. 113.
6. Tyler, II, p. 23.
7. Tyler, II, pp. 24, 25, 34.

criticisms are unfair though. They stop short of seeking an understanding of Wigglesworth and his work, and rather aim merely at turning the reader away from him.

However, recently some scholars have attempted to rescue this once popular poet from the critical shadows cast upon him. In 1968 two anthologies of colonial writing were published, both of which treated Wigglesworth as a major poet, and offered fair comments on his work.[8,9] In 1989 Ronald Bosco edited a scholarly edition of Wigglesworth's poetry, and suggested to his readers that "an open-minded reading of Wigglesworth definitely has its rewards,"[10] calling on them to form their own conclusions, rather than uncritically accepting a body of "inherited opinion." Bosco reviews this inherited opinion, and tries to shed a new light on Wigglesworth's poetry by examining it in the framework of critical standards appropriate to the 17th century, rather than using a standard that would be foreign, and indeed, repugnant to the poet himself.

What Bosco finds is not "a supreme example of theological fire-breathing," but a man "charged with a Puritan teacher's brand of energy and power."[11] He finds not a rude "pulpit thumper," but a man who could effectively speak as a sympathetic spiritual father, as a mediator between God and man, or, when needed, as the "haranguing vitrolic voice of Puritan conscience." "From Wigglesworth's point of view, and from that of several generations of colonials raised on his verse," Bosco writes, "the intentional didactic or sermonic aspect, orthodox content, and plain style of his poetry were its very strengths."[12]

While Bosco proves adept at illuminating the poet's technical accomplishments, he stops short of providing an analysis of where Wigglesworth's work fits into the history of American thought and literature. Such an analysis is, however, essential to any full re-evaluation of Wigglesworth. Earlier critics would have us believe that Wigglesworth was completely irrelevant and unworthy of our consideration. Of course, nothing could be further from the truth. Even if Wigglesworth was the most demented of men, the very popularity of *The Day of Doom* for a century after its publication suggests that it was anything but irrelevant.

In order to gain some insight into *The Day of Doom*'s influence, one must start by understanding some of the factors that went into making it so popular. In the past, the theme of a cold, logical people loving a cold,

---

8. Harrison T. Messerole, ed., *Seventeenth-Century American Poetry* (New York: New York University Press, 1968).
9. Kenneth Silverman, ed., *Colonial American Poetry* (New York: Hafner Publishing Co., 1968).
10. Ronald A. Bosco, ed., *The Poems of Michael Wigglesworth* (Lanham, MD: University Press of America, 1989), p. xviii.
11. Bosco, p. xxi.
12. Bosco, p. xix.

logical poet seems to have sufficed as an explanation. For example, one of Wigglesworth's kinder critics, Kenneth Murdock, in his 1929 edition of *The Day of Doom*, addressed the question as follows:

> "Critic after critic has found in this little volume only brimstone and bad verse. Why, then, its popularity?
> "So far as Wigglesworth's own day is concerned, the answer is easy. The poem presented what was then sound doctrine in a form which, if not satisfying to the most critical in matters of style, was at least in a familiar tradition of popular verse. For a century after 1662 there were many Americans for whom Wigglesworth's theology was still law, and they turned to the poem, as their fathers had done, for the instruction it contained."[13]

Explanations such as this are less than satisfying. Good doctrine and mediocre verse could not make a best-seller today, and they could not in any other age. While the doctrine and the style did not hinder Wigglesworth's poetry—as they might have if they had proven offensive—neither could they alone have propelled it to such heights. Certainly many sermons were preached—and printed—which were both eloquent and correct, yet they never achieved such great fame. Likewise, other Puritan poets did not scale such heights, although what they wrote was quite correct in doctrine. So why did Wigglesworth stand out?

Two factors were involved. Firstly, Wigglesworth brilliantly captured some of the spirit of Puritanism in his work, and nurtured and strengthened that spirit in his readers. Secondly, although the setting of *The Day of Doom* was cosmic, it is not unreasonable to suggest that Wigglesworth was taking high moral ground and attempting to address some of the important issues of his day in the pages of his epic poem.

Wigglesworth and the Issues

To put *The Day of Doom* in proper historical context, we must look back to the earliest struggles to establish a Christian government in North America. When the Puritans came to America, they brought a dream. In England they had faced persecution for seeking to reform the Church of England. They wanted to bring it under the rule of Christ and the Bible, rather than the rule of the king, tradition, and a corrupt clergy. Once in America, the Puritans had the freedom to erect a society based solely on biblical principles. The first Puritans constructed a theocratic government in which only Christians had voting rights, only Christians ruled, and they ruled by applying biblical principles to the law of state.

---

13. Kenneth B. Murdock, ed., *The Day of Doom* (New York: The Spiral Press, 1929), p. vi.

The Puritans also returned the church to the original biblical concept of an *ecclesia*—a body of believers who had been called out from the world by God. In England, the national church was open to all, and in fact often forced upon the citizens. As such, the Church of England consisted of people eager to live holy lives and serve God, as well as those who cared little for God, and who were part of the church for social and political reasons. When the Puritans came to New England, they established spiritual requirements which had to be met before membership would be granted. Typically, candidates for membership had to give testimony as to how God had worked in their lives to bring them to Christ. Next, they would be proposed for membership to the congregation, who would give testimony of the candidate's character, perhaps hear a public confession, and then vote on whether to accept the candidate as a member. If voted into membership, the candidate was called upon to "own the covenant," of the church which was a covenant with God and the other members of the church to "walk . . . in all brotherly love and holy watchfulness to the mutual building up one of another in the fellowship of the Lord Jesus Christ,"[14] thereby submitting to the government of the church, in which the new member would become a participant.

The Puritans had high hopes for their new churches. They believed that by purifying the church, they would succeed in purifying society as a whole, so those who had not come to Christ previously would do so shortly. These hopes were disappointed though. Typical of the times, by 1645 only about one in three people were church members in Boston,[15] even though all were required by law to attend every church service to hear teachings and exhortations. Evidently many never applied for membership, as few who did were turned away.

As the years passed, membership continued to decline. The children of the founders seemed to be losing interest in what their fathers had built. By 1662 the situation had grown so serious that the Massachusetts General Court called a synod to decide what to do. Ther result was the "half-way covenant," a compromise on the requirements for church membership which would admit many more into the church and enlarge its base of members, and thus its authority in the lives of the people.

The half-way covenant was made necessary by earlier compromises in church doctrine. In the early Puritan church, baptism was understood as the seal of God's covenant with His people. It was available only to those members who had owned the covenant, and their children. Although the chidren were not necessarily partakers of saving grace, they were "in a more hopeful way of obtaining regenerating grace" as partakers in the covenant with their parents. As such, baptism was not a sign of salvation,

---

14. Everret Emerson, *Puritanism in America 1620-1750* (Boston:Twayne Publishers, 1977), p. 48.
15. Emerson, p. 55.

but only that salvation would likely come in God's time. However, children who were baptized and granted membership by virture of their parents' experience with God grew up and failed to have similar experiences. Questions about the status of such people in the church loomed large.

The synod of 1662 adopted the proposition that "Church members who were admitted in minority, understanding the doctrine of faith and publicly professing their assent thereto, not scandalous in life and solemnly owning the covenant before the church, wherein they give up themselves and their children to the Lord, and subject themselves to the government of Christ in the church, their children are to be baptized."[16]

This measure gave adults and their children a half-way membership in the church in exchange for their best effort to live Christian lives. In the eyes of some it was a serious compromise of the Christian doctrine of the total depravity of man, since it shifted the essential requriement for church membership and, indirectly, of salvation, away from the question of whether God had imparted His grace, and toward the human works of living a good life and owning the covenant.

Enter Michael Wigglesworth. Born on October 18, 1631, in Yorkshire, England, his family emigrated to New Haven, Connecticut in 1638 when they met with "opposition and persecution for religion" at home. Michael's father, a farmer, saw that his son was not so fit for husbandry as for a more learned occupation, and sent him to school. Michael entered Harvard in 1647, and began to pursue studies in medicine. However, he underwent a profound conversion experience in 1650 or 1651, after which he changed the course of his life to study for the ministry. After graduating first in his class, he remained at Harvard for three years to teach, and then he became the pastor at Malden, Massachusetts, where he remained for the rest of his life.

Shortly after Wigglesworth moved to Malden, he became ill, experiencing a recurring sore throat and weakness that would last thirty years. As a result he was often unable to fulfill his duties as a pastor. This irked the congregation which had just appointed him and added fuel to a controversy which developed when he assumed the pulpit. Wigglesworth's predecessor, Marmaduke Matthews, had implemented more liberal church membership policies and taught liberal and unconventional ideas in the Malden church. When Wigglesworth arrived, young, zealous, and conservative, he was challenged by Matthews' followers. So Wigglesworth found himself in a dilemma. He saw the decline of piety—"declension" as the Puritans called it—in his own congregation, and yet he was too weak to address it effectively. He chose to take up the

---

16. Emerson, p. 87.

pen. In 1658 he wrote an open letter to his congregation to discuss both their declension and his illness. His efforts were successful at quelling the controversy, and by the end of the year his congregation voted to build a new and larger church building.[17]

In 1661, still plagued by illness, Wigglesworth again took up his pen and began work on *The Day of Doom*. He wrote during a time when New England's ministers were everywhere noticing the signs of declension and decreasing church membership. It is not unreasonable to suppose that when Wigglesworth wrote, he was interested not just in writing a doctrinaire poem about the Judgement, but also in attempting to remedy these problems, and speaking to the important issues of his day. He had faced these issues personally in Malden, and he was well aware of what other pastors were experiencing.

In this context, what Wigglesworth wrote was brilliant. Wigglesworth chose not to write a polemic on the issues themselves. Rather he focused on the end result—the Judgement Day—the great hope and fear of every Christian. For indeed, the prize of the Christian is to stand before God on that day and hear "well done, good and faithful servant" and not "depart from Me, you worker of iniquity."[18] Yet, both in the medium he used, and in the subject he chose, Wigglesworth was able to address the problems he saw, while silencing the disputatious.

In writing *The Day of Doom*, Wigglesworth explains that his aim was to lead the unredeemed to "put not off repentance till to morrow"[19] and to "persevere to beg His grace till He thy suit shall hear"[20] as well as to remind the saints to "give up your selves to walk in all His wayes, and study how to live unto His praise."[21] His goal was not to write poetry for the intellectual elite, but to "clearly and familiarly communicate his thoughts to [even] the meanest capacity."[22] So in Wigglesworth's own words, *The Day of Doom* was his effort to check declension in New England.

His solution was not to compromise church standards, but to clarify the issues at hand for his readers, and motivate them to seek God's grace. The real issue was not whether one was numbered as a church member,

17. Richard Crowder, *No Featherbed to Heaven, A Biography of Michael Wigglesworth, 1631-1705* (E. Lansing: Michigan State University Press, 1962), p. 97.
18. And among the Puritans there were enough apocalyptic expectations to make such a topic quite popular. See Joy Gilsdorf, *The Puritan Apocalypse* (New York: Garland Publishing, 1989).
19. Michael Wigglesworth, *A Postscript unto the Reader*, line 299.
20. *Postscript*, lines 357, 358.
21. *Postscript*, lines 407, 408.
22. Murdock, p. vii.

but whether one would be numbered among the elect. Wigglesworth's poem on the Judgement drew the line in matters of right and wrong in a form that the average Puritan could understand.

Although Wigglesworth has been criticized for his severe doctrine, one must understand that he could not have addressed some of these issues without expounding on matters like the fate of babes and unborn children, as well as the fate of those who lived good lives but never found God's redeeming grace. In consigning some of the former[23] and all of the latter[24] to hell, he took the orthodox Calvinist position. Yet it is reasonable to suggest he was also making a statement: Although the church might open its doors to men who live outwardly good lives, such human efforts could buy one nothing in God's sight. Though the church might baptize children of the redeemed and the unredeemed, God still had every right to send them to hell if He so chose. Wigglesworth was fully aware that men are all too ready to follow other men, rather than studying the Bible to find out what is true for themselves. He knew that when the church compromised its doctrine, and admitted members who had not come to a saving knowledge of Christ, men would rest content in that membership and fail to pursue what they needed to be truly saved.[25] The Day of Doom addressed these concerns in no uncertain terms.

Wigglesworth and the Puritan Ideal

So The Day of Doom can be understood not just as a doctrinaire work, but as a poem that was both accessible and relevant to the people of Wigglesworth's day. This may account for a measure of its popularity. Yet Wigglesworth went beyond facing current issues in his poetry. He successfully captured the heart of many Puritans. Although some of his doctrine may seem severe to modern ears, that very doctrine, combined with Wigglesworth's sincere and heartfelt entreaties to make the most of one's time seeking God and finding His grace leave a lasting impression of the Puritan's humility before God. To the Puritan, God was very great, and man was very small. None of man's efforts could buy salvation. Even in his best deeds, done on his own, one would find the taint of sin, and the fallen man of pride. Man's only hope was to humble himself before God, and seek God's enlightenment, mercy and grace. Such humility before a lofty and mighty God was highly prized in Puritan America. At the same

---

23. Michael Wigglesworth, The Day of Doom, 25, 166-176.
24. The Day of Doom, 92-106.
25. The Day of Doom, 114-120.

time, the Puritan believed he should be a light for other men, and his colony a city set upon a hill,[26] that men might see it and come to it in an otherwise dark and gloomy world. So although the Puritan was humble before God, he stood strong and sure among men. Wigglesworth's poem conveys this sense of strength and sureness before the world through its subject matter and firm doctrine.

Yet Wigglesworth does not fit the mold of the "unshrinking rhymer of the five points of Calvinism" in the sense of a throwback to an earlier generation. His work is a good guide to Puritan covenant theology, since it expounds the whole plan of salvation as the Puritans saw it, from the broken covenant of works in Adam to the covenant of grace, of which modern man could partake, and the Puritan understanding of how man can prepare to receive this covenant of grace.

Some have noted the strong neoplatonistic asceticism[27] expressed in Wigglesworth's diary[28], and looked for the same expression in *The Day of Doom*.[29] Apart from the diary, no one would probably question the orthodoxy of *The Day of Doom*. Yet after reading of Wigglesworth's preoccupation with battling his flesh and his sexual desires—the earmarks of neoplatonic asceticism—one has to take a sober second look at his other work within that context, even though the diary ended several years before *The Day of Doom* was begun, and might reasonably be dismissed as a work born of youthful zeal and ignorance.

---

26. John Winthrop, *A Modell of Christian Charity*. This sermon was probably originally deliverd aboard the flagship *Arabella* in 1630 before the Puritans landed. See *Winthrop Papers II* (Boston: Massachusetts Historical Society, 1931).

27. The neoplatonists of ancient Greece and Rome had a dialectical faith, in which the world of forms, or ideas, was set up against the material world of particulars. The material world was considered but a dim shadow of the world of forms, which was somehow more real or true. The neoplatonist often exalted reason as naturally good, and deprecated passion and feeling as inherently evil. The way of salvation for many was thus to mortify the flesh and become a passionless being for whom a detached reason was the mainspring of life. The flesh was the enemy to fight, and the ultimate victory could only be found in death. The result was that the neoplatonist is forever at war with himself: such is the very nature of man in his view. Early Christianity was deeply influenced by neoplatonism. Often the most ludicrous and extreme asceticism was considered to be the height of virtue. Destroying the body, short of suicide, was common practice. This philosophy, although widely practiced for centuries, is contrary to sound theology. Biblically speaking, the entire man, including his intellect, is fallen, not just his flesh. Man's war is with sin (which is often highly intellectual) and not with his body.

28. Edmund S. Morgan, ed., *The Diary of Michael Wigglesworth, 1653-1657* (New York: Harper Torchbooks, 1946).

29. Rousas J. Rushdoony, *The Flight from Humanity, A Study of the Effect of Neoplatonism on Christianity* (Vallecito, CA: Thoburn Press, 1978)

Was the God of *The Day of Doom* simply too rational? and the saints? The Bible pictures God as an emotional being, and the day of judgement as a day of wrath and anger. Yet in *The Day of Doom*, God cooly discourses with sinners and displays little anger, mercy, joy or sorrow. The saints are likewise lacking in feeling in the face of such a great judgement. Certainly some of this was necessary in order for Wigglesworth to present the theological points he wanted to make. However, in the end his God has become more like the passionless ideal of Greece and Rome than the God of the Bible, the Unmoved Mover who governs himself and the universse by reason without reference to feeling.

Likewise, when Christ appears, Wigglesworth's sinners flee from Him and try to hide. Yet once they are translated to the throne and the judgement begins, all are desirous of entering heaven. None vent any hatred of God or exhibit a desire to flee from the Light.[30] Although sucn an approach was necessary for Wigglesworth to get his point across, it is also neoplatonism. The neoplatonist sees the souls of all men as naturally attracted to God, while their flesh turns them away from Him. Only God, forcefully separating Himself from certain souls through judgement, can prevent any from entering heaven and living in His presence.

Finally, Wigglesworth eschews "these delights that gratify the flesh"[31] in typical neoplatonist fashion and uses examples of material desires which led to sin and heartache,

> What gained Sampson by his Delilah?
> What gained David by his Bathsheba?[32]

rather than focusing on the many material blessings which God promised His people for obedience, and the many examples of men so blessed in the Bible.

Many Puritans had a healthy view of God's material blessings in this life. Although they well knew that those blessings could lead them astray from God, they did not shun all material comforts on that basis.[33] However even though most Puritans did not practice the insistent self-abnegation which Wigglesworth reveals in his diary, they were influenced by the neoplatonic view of man, matter and spirit. Certainly Wigglesworth's asceticism did not brand him as a fool in his day. It is probably fair to say that the touch of neoplatonism found in *The Day of Doom* accurately reflected Puritan attitudes. And though many Puritans may not have created such a dispassionate, logical God had they set about rendering the

---

30. Compare with John 3:20.
31. Michael Wigglesworth, *A Postscript Unto the Reader*, l. 222-230.
32. *A Postscript Unto the Reader*, l. 245, 246.
33. William K. Stoever, *A Faire and Easie Way to Heaven* (Middletown, Ct: .
    Wesleyan University Press, 1978) pp. 1-7.

Last Judgement in verse, they obviously found Wigglesworth's account both theologically acceptable and highly moving.

Wigglesworth's neoplatonism puts him in the middle of a movement away from reformation Christianity and back to the earlier Greek world view. To see this, it is important to understand that the essence of neoplatonism is its dialectical view of man, and not how one lives in the light of that dialectic. As such, Wigglesworth, whose theology led him to fight his flesh was not so very different from the enlightenment man, who exalted reason, the romantic, who fled from reason, and the marxist, who sought to bring the social order under the guiding hand of reason. All are trying to deal with the dialectic of form and matter, of reason and the flesh. Wigglesworth's God, who dispassionately condemned men to hell bears a certain resemblance to Nietzsche's superman, who has overcome the last temptation of "fellow suffering," and repudiated any comapssion for man.[34] Following such a line of reasoning, one might argue that Wigglesworth, far from being a stiff defender of orthodoxy, was an innovater who (perhaps unconsciously) helped prepare the way for the acceptance of deism and rationalism in the eighteenth century. Certainly his passionless God is a step away from Calvin's God, and toward the Deists' *deus ex machina*. And certainly he was influential enough that his portrait of God did not fail to mold the thinking of several generations of Americans.

In conclusion, it seems fair to say that, whatever one may think of Wigglesworth, his work cannot be reasonably ignored. Although he may never again be regarded with the respect he had in Puritan New England, neither will he again be disdained and discarded. A dearth of serious scholarship for better than a century has produced a fallow field, which can well reward both the casual reader and the open minded scholar, whether his interest be in art, history, or theology.

---

34. Friedrich Nietzsche, *Thus Spake Zarathustra* (New York: MacMillan Co., 1916), LXXX, p. 401.

On the following Work, and It's Author.

By Jonathan Mitchell

A Verse may find him who a Sermon flies,
Saith *Herbert* well. Great Truths to dress in Meeter;
Becomes a Preacher; who mens Souls doth prize,
That Truth in Sugar roll'd may taste the sweeter.
    No Cost too great, no Care too curious is   5
    To set forth Truth, and win mens Souls to bliss.

In Costly Verse, and most laborious Rymes,
Are dish't up here Truths worthy most regard:
No Toyes, nor Fables (Poets wonted Crimes)
Here be; but things of worth with Wit prepar'd.   10
    Reader, fall too; and if thy tast be good,
    Thou'lt praise the Cook, & say, 'Tis choicest Food.

David 's affliction bred us many a *Psalm*;
From Caves, from mouth of Graves that Singer sweet
Oft tun'd his Soul felt Notes: For not in's Calm,   15
But Storms, to write most Psalms God made him meet;
    Affliction turn'd this Pen to Poetry,
    Whose serious strains do here before thee ly.

This Man with many griefs afflicted sore,
Shut up from speaking much in sickly Cave: 20
Thence painful leisure hath to write the more,
And sends thee Counsels from the mouth o'th' Grave.
    One foot i'th' other World long time hath been:
    Read, and thou'lt say, His heart is all therein.

Yet some (I know) *do judge,*
Mine inability,
To come abroad and do Christ's Work,   35
To be Melancholly;
And that I'm not so weak
As I my self conceit.
But who, in other things have found
Me so conceited yet?   40

   Of who of all my friends,
That have my tryals seen,
Can tell the time in seven years,
When I have dumpish been?
Some think my voice is strong,   45
Most times when I do Preach:
But ten days after what I feel
And suffer, few can reach.

   My prisoned thoughts break forth,
When open'd is the door,   50
Wth greater force and violence,
And strain my voice the more.
But vainly do they tell,
That I am growing stronger,
Who hear me speak in half an hour,   55
Till I can speak no longer.

   Some for, because they see not
My chearfulness to fail,
Nor that I am disconsolate,
Do think I nothing ail.   60
If they had born my griefs,
Their courage might have fail'd them,
And all the Town (perhaps) *have known*
(Once and again) *what ail'd them.*

But why should I complain   65
That have so good a God,
That doth mine heart with comfort fill,
Ev'n whilst I feel his Rod?
In God I have been strong,
When wearied and worn out;   70
And joy'd in him, when twenty woes
Assail'd me round about.

Nor speak I this to boast;
But make Apology
For mine own self and answer those   75
That fail in Charity.
I am (alas) as frail,
Impatient a Creature,
As most that tread upon the ground,
And have as bad a nature.   80

Let God be magnify'd,
Whose everlasting strength
Upholds me under sufferings
Of more than ten years length.
Through whose Almighty pow'r   85
Although I am surrounded
With sorrows more than can be told,
Yet am I not confounded.

For his dear sake have I
This service undertaken,   90
For I am bound to honour Him,
Who hath not me forsaken.
I am a Debtor too,
Unto the sons of Men;
Whom wanting other means, I would   95
Advantage with my Pen.

I would, But (ah!) *my strength,*
When tried, proves so small,
That to the ground without effect,
My wishes often fall.   100
Weak heads, and hands, and states,
Great things cannot produce:
And therefore I this little Piece
Have publish'd for thine use.

Although the thing be small,   105
Yet my good will therein,
Is nothing less than if it had
A larger Volumn been.
Accept it then in Love,
And read it for thy good: 110
There's nothing in't can do thee hurt,
If rightly understood.

The God of Heaven grant
These lines so well to speed,
That thou the things of thine own peace,   115
Through them may'st better heed,
And may'st be stirred up
To stand upon thy guard,
That Death and Judgment may not come,
And find thee unprepar'd   120

Oh get a part of Christ,
And make the Judge thy Friend
So shalt thou be assured of
A happy, glorious end
Thus prayes thy real Friend,   125
And Servant for Christ's Sake,
Who had he strength would not refuse,
    More pains for thee to take.

Michael Wigglesworth.

A Prayer unto Christ The Judge of the World

O Dearest Dread, most glorious King,
I'le of thy justest Judgments sing
Do thou my head and heart inspire,
To Sing aright, as I desire.
Thee, thee alone I'le invocate,   5
For I do much abominate
To call the *Muses* to mine aid:
Which is th' Unchristian use, and trade
Of some that Christians would be thought,
And yet they worship worse then nought.   10
Oh! what a deal of Blasphemy,
And Heathenish Impiety,
In Christian Poets may be found,
Where Heathen gods with praise are Crown'd,
They make *Jehovah* to stand by   15
Till *Juno, Venus, Mercury,*
With frowning *Mars*, and thundering *Jove*
Rule Earth below, and Heaven above.
But I have learnt to pray to none,
Save unto God in Christ alone.   20
Nor will I laud, no, not in jest,
That which I know God doth detest.
I reckon it a damning evil
To give Gods Praises to the Devil.
Thou, *Christ*, art he to whom I pray,   25
Thy Glory fain I would display.
Oh, guide me by thy sacred Sprite
So to indite, and so to write,
That I thine holy Name may praise,
And teach the Sons of men thy wayes.   30

The Day of Doom

1

Still was the night, Serene and Bnght,
    when all Men sleeping lay;
Calm was the season, and carnal reason
    thought so 'twould last for ay.
Soul, take thine ease, let sorrow cease,
    much good thou hast in store:
This was their Song, their Cups among,
    the Evening before.

*The security of the
World before Christ's
coming to Judgement.
Luke 12:19.*

2

Wallowing in all kind of sin,
    vile wretches lay secure:
The best of men had scarcely then
    their Lamps kept in good ure.
Virgins unwise, who through disguise
    amongst the best were number'd,
Had clos'd their eyes; yea, and the wise
    through sloth and frailty slumber'd.

Matt. 25:5.

3

Like as of old, when Men grow bold
    Gods threatnings to contemn,
Who stopt their Ear, and would not hear,
    when Mercy warned them:
But took their course, without remorse,
    til God began to powre
Destruction the World upon
    in a tempestuous showre.

Matt. 24:37, 38.

4

They put away the evil day,
    and drown'd their care and fears,
Till drown'd were they, and swept away
    by vengeance unawares:
So at the last, whilst Men sleep fast   *1 Thess. 5:3.*
    in their security,
Surpriz'd they are in such a snare
    as cometh suddenly.

5

For at midnight brake forth a Light,   *The Suddenness,*
    which turn'd the night to day,   *Majesty, & Terrour of*
And speedily an hideous cry   *Christ's appearing.*
    did all the world dismay.   *Matt. 25:6.*
Sinners awake, their hearts do ake,   *2 Pet. 3:10.*
    trembling their loynes surprizeth;
Amaz'd with fear, by what they hear,
    each one of them ariseth.

6

They rush from Beds with giddy heads,
    and to their windows run,
Viewing this light, which shines more bright
    then doth the Noon-day Sun.   *Matt. 24:29, 30.*
Straightway appears [they see't with tears]
    the Son of God most dread;
 Who with his Train comes on amain
    To Judge both Quick and Dead.

7

Before his face the Heav'ns gave place,
    and Skies are rent asunder,   *2 Pet. 3:10.*
With mighty voice, and hideous noise,
    more terrible than Thunder.
His brightness damps heav'ns glorious lamps
    and makes them hide their heads,
As if afraid and quite dismay'd,
    they quit their wonted steads.

8

Ye sons of men that durst contemn
    the Threatnings of Gods Word.
How cheer you now? your hearts, I trow,
    are thrill'd as with a sword.
Now Atheist blind, whose brutish mind
    a God could never see,
Dost thou perceive, dost now believe
    that Christ thy Judge shall be?

9

Stout Courages, [whose hardiness
    could Death and Hell out-face]
Are you as bold now you behold
    your Judge draw near apace?
They cry, no, no: Alas! and wo!
    our Courage all is gone:
Our hardiness [fool hardiness]
    hath us undone, undone.

10

No heart so bold, but now grows cold
    and almost dead with fear:
No eye so dry, but now can cry,   *Rev. 6:16.*
    and pour out many a tear.
Earths Potentates and pow'rful States,
    Captains and Men of Might,
Are quite abasht, their courage dasht
    at this most dreadful sight.

11

Mean men lament, great men do rent
    their Robes, and tear their hair:
They do not spare their flesh to tear   *Matt. 24:30.*
    through horrible despair.
All Kindreds wail: all hearts do fail:
    horror the world doth fill
With weeping eyes, and loud out-cries,
    yet knows not how to kill.

12

Some hide themselves in Caves and Delves,   *Rev. 6:15, 16.*
    in places under ground:
Some rashly leap into the Deep,
    to scape by being drown'd:
Some to the Rocks [O sensless blocks!]
    and woody Mountains run,
That there they might this fearful sight,
    and dreaded Presence shun.

13

In vain do they to Mountains say,
    Fall on us, and us hide
From Judges ire, more hot than fire,
    for who may it abide?
No hiding place can from his Face,
    sinners at all conceal,
Whose gaming Eyes hid things doth 'spy,
    and darkest things reveal.

14

The Judge draws nigh, exhalted high
    upon a lofty Throne,
Amidst the throng of Angels strong,   *Matt. 25:31.*
    lo, Israel's Holy One!
The excellence of whose presence
    and awful Majesty,
Amazeth Nature, and every Creature,
    doth more than terrify.

15

The Mountains smoak, the Hills are shook   *Rev. 6:14.*
    the Earth is rent and torn,
As if she should be clean dissolv'd,
    or from the Center born.
The Sea doth roar, forsakes the shore,
    and Shrinks away for fear;
The wild Beasts flee into the Sea,
    so soon as he draws near.

16

Whose Glory bright, whose wondrous might,
　　whose Power Imperial,
So far surpass whatever was
　　in Realms Terrestrial;
That tongues of men [nor Angels pen]
　　cannot the same express,
And therefore I must pass it by,
　　lest speaking should transgress.

17

Before his Throne a Trump is blown,
　　Proclaiming th' Day of Doom:
Forthwith he cries, Ye Dead arise,
　　and unto Judgment come.
No sooner said, but 'tis obey'd;
　　Sepulchers open'd are:
Dead Bodies all rise at his call,
　　and's mighty power declare.

1 Thess. 4:16.
Resurrection of the
Dead.
John 5:28, 29.

18

Both Sea and Land, at his Command,
　　their Dead at once surrender:
The Fire and Air constrained are
　　also their dead to tender.
The mighty word of this great Lord
　　links Body and Soul together
Both of the Just, and the unjust,
　　to part no more for ever.

19

The same translates, from Mortal states
　　to Immortality,
All that survive, and be alive,
　　i' th' twinkling of an eye:
That so they may abide for ay
　　to endles weal or woe;
Both the Renate and Reprobate
　　are made to dy no more.

The living Changed.

Luke 20:36.
1 Cor. 15:52.

20

His winged Hosts file through all Coasts,
    together gathering
Both good and bad, both quick and dead,
    and all to Judgment bring.
Out of their holes those creeping Moles,
    that hid themselves for fear,
By force they take, and quickly make
    before the Judge appear.

All brought to
Judgement.
Matt. 24:31.

21

Thus every one before the Throne
    of Christ the Judge is brought,
Both righteous and impious
    that good or ill had wrought.
A separation, and diff'ring station
    by Christ appointed is
[To sinners sad] 'twixt good and bad,
    'twixt Heirs of woe and bliss.

2 Cor. 5:10.
The Sheep separated
from the Goats.
Matt. 25:32.

22

At Christ's right hand the Sheep do stand,
    his holy Martyrs, who
For his dear Name suffering shame,
    calamity and woe,
Like Champions stood, and with their Blood
    their testimony sealed;
Whose innocence without offence,
    to Christ their Judge appealed.

Who are Christ's Sheep.
Matt. 5:10,11.

23

Next unto whom there find a room
    all Christ's afflicted ones,
Who being chastised, neither despised
    nor sank amidst their groans:
Who by the Rod were turn'd to God,
    and loved him the more,
Not murmuring nor quarrelling
    when they were chast'ned sore.

Heb. 12:5, 6, 7.

24

Moreover, such as loved much,
    that had not such a tryal,
As might constrain to so great pain,
    and such deep self denyal:
Yet ready were the Cross to bear,
    when Christ them call'd thereto,
And did rejoyce to hear his voice,
    they're counted Sheep also.

Luke 7:41, 47.

25

Christ's Flock of Lambs there also stands,
    whose Faith was weak, yet true;
All sound Believers [Gospel receivers]
    whose Grace was small, but grew:
And them among an Infant throng
    of Babes, for whom Christ dy'd;
Whom for his own, by wayes unknown
    to men, he sanctify'd.

John 21:15.
Matt. 19:14.
John 3:3.

26

All stand before their Saviour
    in long white Robes yclad,
Their countenance full of pleasance,
    appearing wondrous glad.
O glorious sight! Behold how bright
    dust heaps are made to shine,
Conformed so their Lord unto,
    whose Glory is Divine.

Rev. 6:11.
Phil. 3:21.

27

At Christ's left hand the Goats do stand,
    all whining hypocrites,
Who for self-ends did seem Christ's friends,
    but foster'd guileful sprites;
Who Sheep resembled, but they dissembled
    (their hearts were not sincere);
Who once did throng Christ's Lambs among,
    but now must not come near.

The Goats described, or
the several sorts of
Reprobates on the left
hand.
Matt. 24:51.

28

Apostates and Run-awayes,
    such as have Christ forsaken,
Of whom the Devil, with seven more evil,
    hath fresh possession taken:
Sinners in grain, reserv'd to pain
    and torments most severe:
Because 'gainst light they sinn'd with spight,
    are also placed there.

Luke 11:24, 26.
Heb. 6:4, 5, 6.
Heb. 10:29.

29

There also stand a num'rous band,
    that no Profession made
Of Godliness, nor to redress
    their wayes at all essay'd:
Who better knew, but [sinful Crew]
    Gospel and Law despised;
Who all Christ's knocks withstood like blocks
    and would not be advised.

Luke 12:47.
Prov. 1:24, 26.
John 3:19.

30

Moreover, there with them appear
    a number, numberless
Of great and small, vile wretches all,
    that did Gods Law transgress:
Idolaters, false worshippers,
    Prophaners of Gods Name,
Who not at all thereon did call,
    or took in vain the same.

Gal. 3:10.
1 Cor. 6:9.
Rev. 21:8.

31

Blasphemers lewd, and Swearers shrewd,
    Scoffers at Purity,
That hated God, contemn'd his Rod,
    and lov'd Security;
Sabbath-polluters, Saints persecutors,
    Presumptuous men and proud,
Who never lov'd those that reprov'd;
    all stand amongst this Crowd.

Exod. 20:7, 8.

2 Thess. 1:6, 8, 9.

32

Adulterers and Whoremongers   *Heb. 13:4.*
   where there, with all unchast: *1 Cor. 6:10.*
There Covetous, and Ravenous,
   that Riches got too fast:
Who us'd vile ways themselves to raise
   t' Estates and worldly wealth,
Oppression by, or Knavery,
   by force, or fraud, or stealth.

33

Moreover, there together were
   Children flagitious,
And Parents who did them undo   *Zech. 5:3, 4.*
   by Nurture vicious.   *Gal. 5:19, 20, 21.*
False-witness-bearers, and self-forswearers,
   Murd'rers, and Men of blood,
Witches, Inchanters, and Ale house-haunters,
   beyond account there stood.

34

Their place there find all Heathen blind,
   that Natures light abused,
Although they had no tydings glad,   *Rom. 2:13.*
   of Gospel-grace refused.
There stands all Nations and Generations
   of *Adam's* Progeny,
Whom Christ redeem'd not, who Christ esteem'd not
   through Infidelity.

35

Who no Peace-maker, no Undertaker,   *Acts 4:12.*
   to shrow'd them from Gods ire,
Ever obtain'd; they must be pained
   with everlasting fire.
These num'rous bands, wringing their hands,
   and weeping, all stand there,
Filled with anguish, whose hearts do languish
   through self-tormenting fear.

36

Fast by them stand at Christ's left hand
    the Lion fierce and fell,
The Dragon bold, that Serpent old,
    that hurried Souls to Hell.
There also stand, under command,   *1 Cor. 6:3.*
    Legions of Sprights unclean,
And hellish Fiends, that are no friends
    to God, nor unto Men.

37

With dismal chains, and strongest reins,
    like Prisoners of Hell,
They're held in place before Christ's face,   *Jude 6.*
    till He their Doom shall tell.
These void of tears, but fill'd with fears,
    and dreadful expectation
Of endless pains, and scalding flames,
    stand waiting for Damnation.

38

All silence keep, both Goats and Sheep
    before the Judge's Throne;
With mild aspect to his Elect   *The Saints cleared &*
    then spake the Holy One: *justified.*
My Sheep draw near, your Sentence hear,
    which is to you no dread,
Who clearly now discern, and know
    your sins are pardoned.

39

'Twas meet that ye should judged be,   *2 Cor. 5:10.*
    that so the world may spy   *Eccles. 3:17.*
No cause of grudge, when as I Judge   *John 3:18.*
    and deal impartially.
Know therefore all, both great and small,
    the ground and reason why
These Men do stand at my right hand,
    and look so chearfully.

40

These Men be those my Father chose
   before the worlds foundation,
And to me gave, that I should save
   from Death and Condemnation.
For whose dear sake I flesh did take,
   was of a Woman born
And did inure my self t' indure,
   unjust reproach and scorn.

John 17:6.
Eph. 1:4.

41

For them it was that I did pass
   through sorrows many one:
That I drank up that bitter Cup,
   which made me sigh and groan.
The Cross his pain I did sustain;
   yea more, my Fathers ire
I underwent, my Blood I spent
   to save them from Hell fire.

Rev. 1:5.

42

Thus I esteem'd, thus I redeem'd
   all these from every Nation,
That they may be (as now you see)
   a chosen Generation.
What if ere-while they were as vile,
   as bad as any be,
And yet from all their guilt and thrall
   at once I set them free?

Eph. 2:1, 3.

43

My grace to one is wrong to none:
   none can Election claim
Amongst all those their souls that lose,
   none can Rejection blame.
He that may chuse, or else refuse,
   all men to save or spill,
May this Man chuse, and that refuse,
   redeeming whom he will.

Matt. 20:13, 15.
Rom. 9:20, 21.

44

But as for those whom I have chose   *Isa. 53:4, 5, 11.*
    Salvations heirs to be,
I underwent their punishment,
    and therefore set them free,
I bore their grief, and their relief
    by suffering procur'd,
That they of bliss and happiness
    might firmly be assur'd.

45

And this my grace they did imbrace,   *Acts 13:48.*
    believing on my Name;   *James 2:18.*
Which Faith was true, the fruits do shew   *Heb. 12:7.*
    proceeding from the same: *Matt. 19:29.*
Their Penitence, their Patience,
    their Love and Self-denial
In suffering losses, and bearing Crosses,
    when put upon the tryal.

46

Their sin forsaking, their chearful taking
    my yoke, their Charity
Unto the Saints in all their wants,   *1 John 3:3.*
    and in them unto me.   *Matt. 25:39, 40.*
These things do clear, and make appear
    their Faith to be unfaigned,
And that a part in my desert
    and purchase they have gained.

47

Their debts are paid, their peace is made,
    their sins remitted are;   *Isa. 53:11, 12.*
Therefore at once I do pronounce,   *Rom. 8:16, 17, 33, 34.*
    and openly declare;
That Heav'n is theirs, that they be Heirs   *John 3:18.*
    of Life and of Salvation!
Nor ever shall they come at all
    to Death or to Damnation.

48

Come, Blessed Ones, and sit on Thrones,
    Judging the World with me:
Come, and possess your happiness,
    and bought felicitie.
Henceforth no fears, no care, no tears,
    no sin shall you annoy,
Nor any thing that grief doth bring.
    Eternal Rest enjoy.

Luke 22:29, 30.
Matt. 19:28.

49

You bore the Cross, you suffered loss
    of all for my Names sake:
Receive the Crown that's now your own;
    come, and a Kingdom take.
Thus spake the Judge; the wicked grudge,
    and grind their teeth in vain;
They see with groans these plac't on Thrones
    which addeth to their pain:

Matt. 25:34.
They are placed on
Thrones to joyn with
Christ in judging the
wicked.

50

That those whom they did wrong & slay,
    must now their judgment see!
Such whom they slighted, & once despighted
    must now their Judges be!
Thus 'tis decreed, such is their meed,
    and guerdon glorious!
With Christ they sit, Judging is fit
    to plague the Impious.

1 Cor. 6:2.

51

The wicked are brought to the Bar,
    like guilty Malefactors,
That oftentimes of bloody Crimes
    and Treasons have been Actors.
Of wicked Men, none are so mean
    as there to be neglected:
Nor none so high in dignity,
    as there to be respected.

The wicked brought to
the Bar.
Rom. 2:3, 6, 11.

52

The glorious Judge will priviledge	*Rev. 6:15, 16.*
nor Emperour, nor King:	*Isa. 30:33.*

The glorious Judge will priviledge
    nor Emperour, nor King:
But every one that hath mis-done
    doth unto Judgment bring.
And every one that hath mis-done,
    the Judge impartially
Condemneth to eternal wo,
    and endless misery.

53

Thus one and all, thus great and small,
    the Rich as well as Poor,
And those of place as the most base,
    do stand the Judge before.
They are arraign'd, and there detain'd,
    before Christ's Judgment-seat
With trembling fear, their Doom to hear,
    and feel his angers heat.

54

There Christ demands at all their hands   *Eccles. 11:9; 12:14.*
    a strict and strait account
Of all things done under the Sun,
    whose number far surmount
Man's wit and thought: yet all are brought
    unto this solemn Tryal;
And each offence with evidence,
    so that there's no denial.

55

There's no excuse for their abuses,
    since their own Consciences
More proof give in of each Man's sin,
    than thousand Witnesses,
Though formerly this faculty
    had grosly been abused,
Men could it stifle, or with it trifle,
    when as it them accused.

56

Now it comes in, and every sin
  unto Mens charge doth lay:
It judgeth them, and doth condemn,
  though all the world say nay.
It so stingeth and tortureth,
  it worketh such distress,
That each Man's self against himself,
  is forced to confess.

57

It's vain, moreover, for Men to cover   *Secret sins and works of*
  the least iniquity: *darkness brought to*
The Judge hath seen, and privy been   *light.*
  to all their villany.   *Ps. 139:2, 4, 12.*
He unto light, and open sight   *Rom. 2:16.*
  the works of darkness brings:
He doth unfold both new and old,
  both known and hidden things.

58

All filthy facts, and secret acts,   *Eccles. 12:14.*
  however closly done,
And long conceal'd, are there reveal'd
  before the mid-day Sun.
Deeds of the night shunning the light,
  which darkest corners sought,
To fearful blame, and endless shame,
  are there most justly brought.

59

And as all facts and grosser acts,   *Matt. 12:36.*
  so every word and thought,   *Rom. 7:7.*
Erroneous notion, and lustful motion,
  are unto judgment brought,
No sin so small and trivial
  but hither it must come:
Nor so long past, but now at last
  it must receive a doom.

60

At this sad season, Christ asks a Reason   *An account demanded*
    (with just Austerity)   *of all their actions.*
Of Grace refused, of light abus'd   *John 5:40; 3:19.*
    so oft, so wilfully: *Matt. 25:19, 27.*
Of Talents lent by them mis-spent,
    and on their Lust bestown;
Which if improv'd, as it behov'd,
    Heav'n might have been their own!

61

Of times neglected, of means rejected,
    of God's long-suffering,
And Patience, to Penitence   *Rom. 2:4,5.*
    that sought hard hearts to bring.
Why Cords of love did nothing move
    to shame or to remorse?
Why warnings grave, and counsels, have
    nought chang'd their sinful course?

62

Why chastenings, and evil things,
    why judgments so severe
Prevailed not with them a jot,   *Isa. 1:5.*
    nor wrought an awful fear?
Why Promises of Holiness,   *Jer. 2:20.*
    and new Obedience,
They oft did make, but always brake
    the same, to God's offence?

63

Why still Hell-ward, without regard,
    they boldly ventured,   *John 3:19, 20.*
And chose Damnation before Salvation,   *Prov. 8:36.*
    when it was offered?   *Luke 12:20, 21.*
Why sinful pleasures, & earthly treasures,
    like fools, they prized more
Than heav'nly wealth, Eternal health,
    and all Christ's Royal store?

64

Why, when he stood offring his Blood
    to wash them from their sin,
They would embrace no saving Grace,
    but liv'd and dy'd therein?
Such aggravations, where no evasions,
    no false pretences hold,
Exaggerate and cumulate
    guilt more than can be told.

Luke 13:34.
John 5:40; 15:22.

65

They multiply and magnify
    mens gross iniquities,
They draw down wrath (as Scripture saith)
    out of Gods treasuries
Thus all their ways Christ open lays
    to men and Angels view,
And, as they were, makes them appear
    in their own proper hew.

66

Thus he doth find of all Mankind,
    that stand at his left hand,
No Mothers Son, but hath mis-done,
    and broken God's Command.
All have transgrest, even the best,
    and merited God's wrath
Unto their own perdition,
    and everlasting scath.

Rom. 3:10, 12.

67

Earths dwellers all, both great and small,
    have wrought iniquity,
And suffer must, for it is just,
    Eternal misery.
Amongst the many there come not any,
    before the Judge's face,
That able are themselves to clear,
    of all this cursed race.

Rom. 6:23.

68

Nevertheless, they all express,
    Christ granting liberty,
What for their way they have to say,
    how they have liv'd, and why.
They all draw near, and seek to clear
    themselves by making pleas.
There Hypocrites, false-hearted wights,
do make such pleas as these.

*Hypocrites plead for
themselves.*

69

Lord, in thy Name, and by the same,
    we Devils dispossest,
We rais'd the dead, and ministred
    succour to the distrest.
Our painful teaching, & pow'rful preaching
    by thine own wondrous might,
Did throughly win to God from sin
    many a wretched wight.

Matt. 7:21, 22, 23.

70

All this, quoth he, may granted be,
    and your case little better'd,
Who still remain under a chain,
    and many irons fetter'd.
You that the dead have quickened,
    and rescu'd from the grave,
Your selves were dead, yet never ned,
    a Christ your Souls to save.

*The judge replyeth.
John 6:70.
1 Cor. 9:27.*

71

You that could preach, and others teach
    what way to life doth lead;
Why were you slack to find that track,
    and in that way to tread?
How could you bear to see or hear
    of others freed at last,
From Satan's pawes whilst in his jawes
    your selves were held more fast?

Rom. 2:19, 21, 22, 23.

72

Who though you knew Repentance true,
    and Faith in my great Name,
The only mean to quit you clean,
    from punishment and blame,
Yet took no pain true Faith to gain,
    such as might not deceive,
Nor would repent, with true intent,
    your evil deeds to leave.

John 9:41.

Rev. 2:21, 22.

73

His Masters will how to fulfill
    the servant that well knew,
Yet left undone his duty known,
    more plagues to him are due.
You against light perverted right;
    wherefore it shall be now
For Sidon and for Sodoms Land
    more easie than for you.

Luke 12:47.
Matt. 11:21, 22, 24.

74

But we have in thy presence been,
    say some, and eaten there.
Did we not eat thy Flesh for meat,
    and feed on heavenly Cheer?
Whereon who feed shall never need,
    as thou thy self dost say,
Nor shall they dy eternally,
    but live with Christ for ay.

Another plea of
hypocrites.
Luke 13:26.

75

We may alledge, thou gav'st a pledge
    of thy dear love to us
In Wine and Bread, which figured
    thy Grace bestowed thus.
Of strengthning Seals, of sweetest Meals,
    have we so oft partaken;
And shall we be cast off by thee,
    and utterly forsaken?

76

To whom the Lord thus in a word
    returns a short reply,
I never knew any of you
    that wrought iniquity.
You say y'have been my Presence in:
    but friends, how came you there
With Raiment vile that did defile
    and quite disgrace my Cheer?

Is Answered.
Luke 13:27.
Matt. 22:12.

77

Durst you draw near without due fear
    unto my holy Table?
Durst you prophane, and render vain
    so far as you were able,
Those Mysteries? which whoso prize
    and carefully improve
Shall saved be undoubtedly,
    and nothing shall them move.

78

How durst you venture, bold guests, to enter
    in such a sordid hew,
Amongst my guests, unto those Feasts
    that were not made for you?
How durst you eat for spiritual meat
    your bane, and drink damnation,
Whilst by your guile you rendred vile
    so rare and great Salvation?

1 Cor. 11:27, 29.

79

Your fancies fed on heav'nly Bread,
    your hearts fed on some Lust:
You lov'd the Creature more than th' Creator,
    your Souls clave to the dust.
And think you by Hypocrisie,
    and cloaked Wickedness,
To enter in, laden with sin,
    to lasting happiness?

Matt. 6:21, 24.
Rom. 1:25.

80

This your excuse shews your abuse   *1 Cor. 11:27, 29.*
    of things ordain'd for good;
And doth declare you guilty are
    of my dear Flesh and Blood.
Wherefore those Seals and precious Meals
    you put so much upon
As things divine, they seal and sign
    you to Perdition.

81

Then forth issue another Crew
    (those being silenced)
Who drawing nigh to the most High   *Another sort of*
    adventure thus to plead: *hypocrites make their*
We sinners were, say they, it's clear,   *pleas.*
    deserving Condemnation:
But did not we rely on thee,
    O Christ, for whole Salvation?

82

We did believe and oft receive
    thy gracious promises:
We took great care to get a share   *Acts 8:13.*
    in endless happiness.   *Isa. 58:2, 3.*
We pray'd & wept, we Fast-dayes kept,   *Heb. 64:5.*
    lewd ways we did eschew:
We joyful were thy Word to hear;
    we form'd our lives anew.

83

We thought our sin had pard'ned been;
    that our Estate was good,
Our debts all paid, our peace well made,
    our Souls wash'd with thy Blood.
Lord, why dost thou reject us now,   *2 Pet. 2:20.*
    who have not thee rejected,
Nor utterly true sanctity
    and holy life neglected,

84

The Judge incensed at their pretenced
    self-vanting Piety,
With such a look as trembling strook
    into them, made reply;
O impudent, impenitent,
    and guileful generation!
Think you that I cannot descry
    your hearts abomination?

The Judge uncaseth
them.

John 2:24, 25.

85

You nor receiv'd, nor yet believ'd
    my Promises of Grace;
Nor were you wise enough to prize
    my reconciled Face:
But did presume that to assume
    which was not yours to take,
And challenged the Childrens bread,
    yet would not sin forsake.

John 6:64.

Ps. 50:16.
Matt. 15:26.

86

Being too bold you laid fast hold,
    where int'rest you had none,
Your selves deceiving by your believing,
    all which you might have known,
You ran away, but ran astray,
    with Gospel-promises,
And perished; being still dead
    in sins and trespasses.

Rev. 3:17.

Matt. 13:20.

87

How oft did I Hypocrisie
    and Hearts deceit unmask
Before your sight, giving you light
    to know a Christians task?
But you held fast unto the last
    your own Conceits so vain:
No warning could prevail, you would
    your own Deceits retain.

Matt. 6:2, 4, 24.
Jer. 8:5, 6, 7, 8.

88

As for your care to get a share
   in bliss; the fear of Hell,
And of a part in endless smart,   *Ps. 78:34, 35, 36, 37.*
   did thereunto compell.
Your holiness and ways redress,
   such as it was, did spring
From no true love to things above,
   but from some other thing.

89

You pray'd & wept, you Fast-days kept;   *Zech. 7:5, 6.*
   but did you this to me?   *Isa. 58:3, 4.*
No, but for sin, you sought to win,   *1 Sam. 15:13, 21.*
   the greater libertie.   *Isa. 1:11, 15.*
For all your vaunts, you had vile haunts,
   for which your Consciences
Did you alarm, whose voice to charm
   you us'd these practices.

90

Your Penitence, your diligence
   to Read, to Pray, to Hear,   *Matt. 6:2, 5.*
Were but to drown'd the damorous sound   *John 5:44.*
   of Conscience in your ear.
If light you lov'd, vain glory mov'd
   your selves therewith to store,
That seeming wise, men might you prize,
   and honour you the more.

91

Thus from your selves unto your selves,
   your duties all do tend: *Zech. 7:5, 6.*
And as self-love the wheels doth move,   *Hos. 10:1.*
   so in self-love they end
Thus Christ detects their vain projects,
   and close Impiety,
And plainly shews that all their shows
   were but Hypocrisy.

92

Then were brought nigh a Company
    of Civil honest Men,
That lov'd true dealing, and hated stealing,
    ne'r wrong'd their Bretheren;
Who pleaded thus, Thou knowest us
    that we were blameless livers;
No Whoremongers, no Murderers,
    no quarrellers nor strivers.

Civil honest mens pleas.
Luke 18:11.

93

Idolaters, Adulterers,
    Church-robbers we were none,
Nor false-dealers, no couzeners,
    but paid each man his own.
Our way was fair, our dealing square,
    we were no wastful spenders,
No lewd toss-pots, no drunken sots,
    no scandalous offenders,

94

We hated vice, and set great price,
    by vertuous conversation:
And by the same we got a name,
    and no small commendation.
God's Laws express that righteousness,
    is that which he doth prize;
And to obey, as he doth say,
    is more than sacrifice.

1 Sam. 15:22.

95

Thus to obey, hath been our way;
    let our good deeds, we pray,
Find some regard and some reward
    with thee, O Lord, this day.
And whereas we transgressors be,
    of *Adam's* Race were none,
No not the best, but have confest
    themselves to have mis-done.

Eccles. 7:20.

96

Then answered unto their dread,
　the Judge: True Piety
God doth desire and eke require
　no less than honesty.
Justice demands at all your hands
　perfect Obedience:
If but in part you have come short,
　that is a just offence.

Are taken off & rendred
invalid.
Deut. 10:12.
Titus 2:12.
James 2:10.

97

On Earth below, where men did ow
　a thousand pounds and more,
Could twenty pence it recompence?
　could that have clear'd the score?
Think you to buy felicity
　with part of what's due debt?
Or for desert of one small part,
　the whole should off be set?

98

And yet that part, whose great desert
　you think to reach so far
For your excuse, doth you accuse,
　and will your boasting mar.
However fair, however square,
　your way and work hath been,
Before mens eyes, yet God espies
　iniquity therein.

Luke 18:11, 14.

99

God looks upon th' affection
　and temper of the heart;
Not only on the action,
　and the external part.
Whatever end vain men pretend,
　God knows the verity;
And by the end which they intend
　their words and deeds doth try.

1 Sam. 16:7.
2 Chron. 25:2.

100

Without true Faith, the Scripture saith   *Heb. 11:6.*
   God cannot take delight
In any deed, that doth proceed
   from any sinful wight.
And without love all actions prove   *1 Cor. 13:1, 2, 3.*
   but barren empty things.
Dead works they be, and vanitie,
   the which vexation brings.

101

Nor from true faith, which quencheth wrath
   hath your obedience flown:
Nor from true love, which wont to move
   Believers hath it grown.
Your argument shews your intent,
   in all that you have done:
You thought to scale Heav'ns lofty Wall
   by Ladders of your own.

102

Your blinded spirit, hoping to merit   *Rom. 10:3.*
   by your own Righteousness,
Needed no Saviour, but your behaviour,
   and blameless carriages
You trusted to what you could do,
   and in no need you stood:
Your haughty pride laid me aside,
   and trampled on my Blood.

103

All men have gone astray, and done,
   that which Gods Laws condemn:
But my Purchase and offered Grace
   all men did not contemn.   *Rom. 9:30, 32.*
The *Ninevites*, and *Sodomites*,   *Matt. 11:23, 24; 12:41.*
   had no such sin as this:
Yet as if all your sins were small,
   you say, All did amiss.

104

Again you thought and mainly sought   *Matt. 6:5.*
    a name with men t'acquire;
Pride bare the Bell, that made you swell,
    and your own selves admire.
Mean fruit it is, and vile, I wiss,
    that springs from such a root:
Vertue divine and genuine
    wonts not from pride to shoot.

105

Such deeds as your are worse than poor:
    they are but sins guilt over
With silver dross, whose glistering gloss   *Prov. 26:23.*
    can them no longer cover.   *Matt. 23:27.*
The best of them would you condemn,
    and ruine you alone,
Although you were from faults so clear,
    that other you had none.

106

Your Gold is brass, your silver dross,   *Prov. 15:8.*
    your righteousness is sin: *Rom. 3:20.*
And think you by such honesty
    eternal life to win?
You much mistake, if for its sake
    you dream of acceptation;
Whereas the same deserveth shame,
    and meriteth Damnation.

107

A wond'rous Crowd then 'gan aloud,   *Those that pretend want*
    thus for themselves to say,   *of opportunity to repent.*
We did intend, Lord to amend,   *Prov. 27:1.*
    and to reform our way: *James 4:13.*
Our true intent was to repent,
    and make our peace with thee;
But sudden death stopping our breath,
    left us no libertie.

108

Short was our time, for in his prime
    our youthful flow'r was cropt:
We dy'd in youth, before full growth,
    so was our purpose stopt.
Let our good will to turn from ill,
    and sin to have forsaken,
Accepted be, O Lord, by thee,
    and in good part be taken.

109

To whom the Judge: where you alledge   *Are Confuted and*
    the shortness of the space,   *Convicted.*
That from your birth you liv'd on earth,   *Eccles. 12:1.*
    to compass saving Grace: *Rev. 2:21.*
It was Free grace that any space
    was given you at all
To turn from evil, defie the Devil,
    and upon God to call.

110

One day, one week, wherein to seek   *Luke 13:24.*
    God's face with all your hearts,   *2 Cor. 6:2.*
A favour was that far did pass   *Heb. 3:7, 8, 9.*
    the best of your deserts.
You had a season, what was your reason
    such precious hours to waste?
What could you find, what could you mind
    that was of greater haste?

111

Could you find time for vain pastime,
    for loose licentious mirth?
For fruitless toyes, and fading joyes   *Eccles. 11:9.*
    that perish in the birth?   *Luke 14:18, 19, 20.*
Had you good leasure for carnal Pleasure,
    in dayes of health and youth?
And yet no space to seek God's face,
    and turn to him in truth?

112

In younger years, beyond your fears,
    what if you were surprised?
You put away the evil day,
    and of long life devised.
You oft were told, and might behold,
    that Death no Age doth spare;
Why then did you your time foreslow,
    and slight your Souls welfare?

Amos 6:3, 4, 5, 6.

Eph. 5:16.
Luke 19:42.

113

Had your intent been to repent,
    and had you it desir'd,
There would have been endeavours seen,
    before your time expir'd.
God makes no treasure, nor hath he pleasure
    in idle purposes:
Such fair pretences are foul offences,
    and cloaks for wickedness,

Luke 13:24, 25, &c.

Phil. 2:12.

114

Then were brought in, and charg'd with sin,
    another Company,
Who by Petition obtain'd permission,
    to make Apology:
They argues, We were misled,
    as is well known to thee,
By their Example, that had more ample
    abilities than we:

Some plead Examples
of their betters.
Matt. 18:7.

115

Such as profest they did detest,
    and hate each wicked way:
Whose seeming grace whilst we did trace,
    our Souls were led astray.
When men of Parts, Learning and Arts,
    Professing Piety,
Did thus and thus, it seem'd to us
    we might take liberty.

John 7:48.

116

The Judge replies, I gave you eyes,
    and light to see your way,
Which had you lov'd, and well improv'd
    you had not gone astray.
My Word was pure, the Rule was sure,
    why did you it forsake,
Or thereon trample, and mens example,
    your Directory make?

Who are told that
Examples are no Rules.

Ps. 19:8, 11.
Exod. 23:2.
Ps. 50:17, 18.

117

This you well knew, that God is true
    and that most men are liars,
In word professing holiness,
    in deed thereof deniers.
O simple fools! that having Rules
    your lives to regulate,
Would then refuse, and rather chuse
    vile men to imitate.

2 Tim. 3:5.

118

But Lord, say they, we went astray,
    and did more wickedlie,
By means of those whom thou hast chose
    Salvation heirs to be.
To whom the Judge: What you alledge,
    doth nothing help the case;
But makes appear how vile you were,
    and rend'reth you more base.

They urge that they were
misled by godly mens
Example: But all their
shifts turn to their
greater shame.
1 Cor. 11:1.

119

You understood that what was good,
    was to be followed,
And that you ought that which was naught
    to have relinquished.
Contrariwayes, it was your guise,
    only to imitate
Good mens defects, and their neglects
    that were regenerate.

Phil. 4:8.

120

But to express their holiness,
    or imitate their grace,
You little car'd, nor once prepar'd   *Ps. 32:5.*
    your hearts to seek my face.   *2 Chron. 32:26.*
They did repent, and truly rent   *Matt. 26:75.*
    their hearts for all known sin: *Prov. 1:24, 25.*
You did offend, but not amend,
    to follow them therein.

121

We had thy Word, say some, O Lord,   *Some plead the*
    but wiser men than we   *Scriptures darkness.*
Could never yet interpret it,   *And difference amongst*
    but always disagree.   *Interpreters.*
How could we fools be led by Rules,   *2 Pet. 3:16.*
    so far beyond our ken,
Which to explain did so much pain,
    and puzzle wisest men?

122

Was all my word abstruse and hard?
    the Judge then answered: *They are confuted.*
It did contain much truth so plain,   *Prov. 14:6.*
    you might have run and read,   *Isa. 35:8.*
But what was hard you never car'd   *Hos. 8:12.*
    to know nor studied.
And things that were most plain and clear
    you never practised.

123

The Mystery of Pietie   *Matt. 11:25.*
    God unto Babes reveals;
When to the wise he it denies,
    and from the world conceals.
If to fulfil Gods holy will   *Prov. 2:3, 4, 5.*
    had seemed good to you
You would have sought light as you ought,
    and done the good you knew.

124

Then came in view another Crew,
    and 'gan to make their pleas;
Amongst the rest, some of the best
    had such poor shifts as these:
Thou know'st right well, who all canst tell
    we liv'd amongst thy foes,
Who the Renate did sorely hate,
    and goodness much oppose.

Others the fear of
Persecution.
Acts 28:22.

125

We holiness durst not profess,
    fearing to be forlorn
Of all our friends, and for amends
    to be the wickeds scorn.
We knew their anger would much endanger
    our lives, and our estates:
Therefore for fear we dust appear
    no better than our mates.

126

To whom the Lord returns this word;
    O wonderful deceits!
To cast off aw of Gods strict Law,
    and fear mens wrath and threats.
To fear hell-fire and Gods fierce ire
    less than the rage of men,
As if Gods wrath, could do less scath
    than wrath of bretheren.

They are answered.

Luke 12:4, 5.
Isa. 51:12, 13.

127

To use such strife, a temporal life,
    to rescue and secure,
And be so blind as not to mind
    that life that will endure.
This was your case, who carnal peace
    more than true joyes did favour;
Who fed on dust, clave to your lust,
    and spurned at my favour.

128

To please your kin, mens love to win,
    to flow in worldly wealth,
To save your skin, these things have bin
    more than Eternal health.
You had your choice, wherein rejoyce,
    it was your portion,
For which you chose your Souls t' expose
    unto perdition.

Luke 9:23, 24, 25;
16:25.

129

Who did not hate friends, life, and state,
    with all things else for me.
And all forsake, and's Cross up-take,
    shall never happy be.
Well worthy they to dye for ay,
    who death then life had rather.
Death is their due, that so value
    the friendship of my Father.

Luke 9:26.
Prov. 8:36.
John 3:19, 20.

130

Others Argue, and not a few,
    is not God gracious?
His Equity and Clemency
    are they not marvellous?
Thus we believ'd; are we deceiv'd?
    cannot his mercy great,
(As hath been told to us of old)
    asswage his angers heat?

Others plead for
Pardon both from Gods
mercy and justice.
Ps. 78:38.

131

How can it be that God should see
    his Creatures endless pain,
Or hear the groans and rueful moans,
    and still his wrath retain?
Can it agree with Equitie?
    can mercy have the heart
To recompence few years offence
    with Everlasting smart?

2 Kings 14:26.

132

Can God delight in such a sight
    as sinners misery?
Or what great good can this our blood
    bring unto the most High?
Oh, thou that dost thy Glory most   *Ps. 30:9.*
    in pard'ning sin display!
Lord, might it please thee to release,   *Mic. 7:18.*
    and pardon us this day?

133

Unto thy Name more glorious fame
    would not such mercy bring?
Would not it raise thine endless praise,
    more than our suffering?
With that they cease, holding their peace,
    but cease not still to weep;
Grief ministers a flood of tears,
    in which their words do steep.

134

But all too late, griefs out of date,
    when life is at an end.
The glorious King thus answering,
    all to his voice attend:
God gracious is, quoth he, like his   *They answered.*
    no mercy can be found;
His Equity and Clemency
    to sinners do abound.

135

As may appear by those that here   *Mercy that now shines*
    are plac'd at my right hand;   *forth in the vessels of*
Whose stripes I bore, and clear'd the score, *Mercy.*
    that they might quitted stand.
For surely none, but God alone,   *Mic. 7:18.*
    whose Grace transcends mens thought, *Rom. 9:23.*
For such as those that were his foes
    like wonders would have wrought.

136

And none but he such lenitee
   and patience would have shown
To you so long, who did him wrong,
   and pull'd his judgments down.
How long a space (O stiff neck'd race)
   did patience you afford?
How oft did love you gently move,
   to turn unto the Lord?

Did also long wait
upon such as abused it.

Rom. 2:4.
Hos. 11:4.

137

With Cords of love God often strove
   your stubborn hearts to tame:
Nevertheless your wickedness,
   did still resist the same.
If now at last Mercy be past
   from you for evermore,
And Justice come in Mercies room,
   yet grudge you not therefore.

Luke 13:34.
The day of Grace now
past.

138

If into wrath God turned hath
   his long long suffering,
And now for love you vengeance prove,
   it is an equal thing.
Your waxing worse, hath stopt the course
   of wonted Clemency:
Mercy refus'd, and Grace misus'd,
   call for severity.

Luke 19:42, 43.
Jude 4.

139

It's now high time that ev'ry Crime
   be brought to punishment:
Wrath long contain'd, and oft restrain'd,
   at last must have a vent:
Justice severe cannot forbear
   to plague sin any longer,
But must inflict with hand most strict
   mischief upon the wronger.

Rom. 2:5, 6.
Isa. 1:24.
Amos 2:13.
Gen. 18:25.

140

In vain do they for Mercy pray,   *Matt. 25:3, 11, 12.*
    the season being past,   *Prov. 1:28, 29, 30.*
Who had no care to get a share
    therein, while time did last.
The man whose ear refus'd to hear
    the voice of Wisdoms cry,
Earn'd this reward, that none regard
    him in his misery.

141

It doth agree with equity,
    and with Gods holy Law,   *Isa. 5:18, 19.*
That those should dye eternally   *Gen. 2:17.*
    that death upon them draw.   *Rom. 2:8, 9.*
The Soul that sins damnation wins,
    for so the Law ordains;
Which Law is just, and therefore must
    such suffer endless pain[s].

142

Eternal smart is the desert,   *Rom. 6:23.*
    ev'n of the least offence;   *2 Thess. 1:8, 9.*
Then wonder not if I allot
    to you this Recompence:
But wonder more, that since so sore
    and lasting plagues are due
To every sin, you liv'd therein,
    who well the danger knew.

143

God hath no joy to crush or 'stroy,   *Ezek. 33:11.*
    and ruine wretched wights,   *Exod. 34:7; 14:17.*
But to display the glorious Ray   *Rom. 9:22.*
    of Justice he delights.
To manifest he doth detest,
    and throughly hate all sin,
By plaguing it as is most fit,
    this shall him glory win.

144

Then at the Bar arraigned are
  an impudenter sort,
Who to evade the guilt that's laid
  upon them, thus retort;
How could we cease thus to transgress?
  how could we Hell avoid,
Whom Gods Decree shut out from thee,
  and sign'd to be destroy'd?

Some pretend they were
shut out from Heaven
by Gods Decree.
Rom. 9:18, 19.

145

Whom God ordains to endless pains,
  by Law unalterable,
Repentence true, Obedience new,
  to save such are unable:
Sorrow for sin, no good can win,
  to such as are rejected;
Ne can they grieve, nor yet believe,
  that never were elected.

Heb. 22:17.
Rom. 11:7, 8.

146

Of Man's fall'n Race, who can true Grace,
  or Holiness obtain?
Who can convert or change his heart,
  if God withhold the same?
Had we apply'd our selves, and try'd
  as much as who did most
God's love to gain, our busie pain
  and labour had been lost.

147

Christ readily makes this Reply,
  I damn you not because
You are rejected, or not elected,
  but you have broke my Laws:
It is but vain your wits to strain,
  the end and means to sever:
Men fondly seek to part or break
  what God hath link'd together.

Their pleas taken off.

Luke 13:27.
2 Pet. 1:9, 10 compared
with Matt. 19:6.

148

Whom God will save, such he will have,   *Acts 3:19; 16:31.*
    the means of life to use: *1 Sam. 2:15.*
Whom he'll pass by, shall chuse to dy,   *John 3:19.*
    and ways of life refuse.   *John 5:40.*
He that fore-sees, and fore-decrees,   *2 Thess. 2:11, 12.*
    in wisdom order'd has,
That man's free-will electing ill,
    shall bring his will to pass.

149

High God's Decree, as it is free,   *Ezek. 33:11, 12, 13.*
    so doth it none compel   *Luke 13:34.*
Against their will to good or ill,   *Prov. 8:33, 36.*
    it forceth none to Hell.
They have their wish whose Souls perish
    with Torments in Hell-fire,
Who rather chose their Souls to lose,
    than leave a loose desire.

150

God did ordain sinners to pain   *Gen. 2:17.*
    and I to Hell send none,   *Matt. 25:41, 42.*
But such as swerv'd, and have deserv'd   *Ezek. 18:20.*
    destruction as their own.
His pleasure is, that none from bliss
    and endless happiness
Be barr'd, but such as wrong'd him much
    by wilful wickedness.

151

You, sinful Crew, no other knew
    but you might be elect;
Why did you then your selves condemn?   *2 Pet. 1:10.*
    why did you me reject?   *Acts 13:46.*
Where was your strife to gain that life   *Luke 13:24.*
    which lasteth evermore?
You never knock'd, yet say God lock'd
    against you Heav'ns door.

152

'Twas no vain task to knock, to ask,
    whilst life continued.
Whoever sought heav'n as he ought,
    and seeking perished?
The lowly meek who truly seek
    for Christ, and for Salvation,
There's no Decree whereby such be
    ordain'd to Condemnation.

Matt. 7:7, 8.

Gal. 5:22, 23.

153

You argue than; But abject men,
    whom God resolves to spill,
Cannot repent, nor their hearts rent;
    ne can they change their will.
Not for his *Can* is any man
    adjudged into Hell:
But for his *Will* to do what's ill,
    and nilling to do well.

John 3:19.

154

I often stood tend'ring my Blood
    to wash away your guilt:
And eke my Spright to frame you right,
    lest your Souls should be split.
But you vile Race, rejected Grace,
    when Grace was freely proffer'd:
No changed heart, no heav'nly part
    would you, when it was offer'd.

John 5:40.

155

Who wilfully the Remedy,
    and means of life contemned,
Cause have the same themselves to blame,
    if now they be condemned.
You have your selves, you and none else,
    your selves have done to dy.
You chose the way to your decay,
    and perisht wilfully.

John 15:22, 24.
Heb. 2:3.
Isa. 66:3, 4.

156

These words appall and daunt them all;
    dismai'd, and all amort,
Like stocks they stand at Christ's left-hand,
    and dare no more retort.
Then were brought near with trembling fear,
    a number numberless
Of blind Heathen, and brutish men,
    that did Gods Laws transgress.

157

Whose wicked ways Christ open layes,
    and makes their sins appear,
They making pleas their case to ease,
    if not themselves to clear.
Thy written Word (say they) good Lord,
    we never did enjoy:
We nor refus'd, nor it abus'd;
    Oh, do not us destroy!

*Heathen men plead
want of the written
Word.*

158

You ne'r abus'd, nor yet refus'd
    my written Word, you plead,
That's true (quoth he) therefore shall ye
    the less be punished.
You shall not smart for any part
    of other mens offence,
But for your own transgression
    receive due recompence.

*Matt. 11:22.
Luke 12:48.*

159

But we were blind, say they, in mind,
    too dim was Natures Light,
Our only guide, as hath been try'd
    to bring us to the sight
Of our estate degenerate
    and curst by *Adam's* Fall;
How we were born and lay forlorn
    in bondage and in thrall.

*1 Cor. 1:21.
And insufficiency of the
Light of Nature.*

160

We did not know a Christ till now,
    nor how faln man be saved,
Else would we not, right well we wot,
    have so our selves behaved.
We should have mourn'd, we should have turn'd
    from sin at thy Reproof,
And been more wise through thy advice,
    for our own Souls behoof.

161

But Natures Light shin'd not so bright
    to teach us the right way:
We might have lov'd it, and well improv'd,   *They are answered.*
    and yet have gone astray.
The Judge most High makes this Reply,
    you ignorance pretend,
Dimness of sight, and want of light
    your course Heav'nward to bend.

162

How came your mind to be so blind?   *Gen. 1:27.*
    I once you knowledge gave,   *Eccles. 7:29.*
Clearness of sight, and judgment right;   *Heb. 13:9.*
    who did the same deprave?
If to your cost you have it lost,
    and quite defac'd the same;
Your own desert hath caus'd the Smart,
    you ought not me to blame.

163

Your selves into a pit of woe,   *Matt. 11:25 compared*
    your own transgression led: *with 20 & 15.*
If I to none my Grace had shown,
    who had been injured?
If to a few, and not to you,
    I shew'd a way of life,
My Grace so free, you clearly see,
    gives you no ground of strife.

164

'Tis vain to tell, you wot full well
　　if you in time had known
Your Misery and Remedy,
　　your actions had it shown.
You, sinful Crew, have not been true   *Rom. 1:20, 21, 22.*
　　unto the Light of Nature,
Nor done the good you understood,
　　nor owned your Creator.

165

He that the Light, because 'tis Light,
　　hath used to despize,
Would not the Light shining more bright,   *Rom. 2:12, 25; 1:32.*
　　be likely for to prize.
If you had lov'd, and well improv'd   *Matt. 12:41.*
　　your knowledge and dim sight,
Herein your pain had not been vain,
　　your plagues had been more light.

166

Then to the Bar, all they drew near   *Reprobate infants plead*
　　who dy'd in Infancy,   *for themselves.*
And never had or good or bad   *Rev. 20:12, 15*
　　effected pers'nally,   *Compared with*
But from the womb unto the tomb   *Rom. 5:12, 14; 9:11, 13.*
　　were straightway carried,
(Or at the last e're they transgrest)
　　who thus began to plead:

167

If for our own transgression,   *Ezek. 18:2.*
　　or disobedience,
We here did stand at thy left-hand
　　just were the Recompence:
But *Adam's* guilt our souls hath split,
　　his fault is charg'd on us;
And that alone hath overthrown,
　　and utterly undone us.

168

Not we, but he, ate of the tree
    whose fruit was interdicted:
Yet on us all of his sad Fall,
    the punishment's inflicted.
How could we sin that had not been
    or how is his sin our
Without consent, which to prevent,
    we never had a pow'r?

169

O great Creator, why was our Nature
    depraved and forlorn?
Why so defil'd, and made so vild
    whilst we were yet unborn?
If it be just, and needs we must
    transgressors reck'ned be,
Thy Mercy, Lord, to us afford,   *Ps. 51:5.*
    which sinners hath set free.

170

Behold we see *Adam* set free,
    and sav'd from his trespass,
Whose sinful Fall hath split us all,
    and brought us to this pass.
Canst thou deny us once to try,
    or Grace to us to tender,
When he finds grace before thy face,
    that was the chief offender?

171

Then answered the Judge most dread,   *Their Argument taken*
    God doth such doom forbid,   *off.*
That men should dye eternally   *Ezek. 18;20.*
    for what they never did.   *Rom. 5:12, 19.*
But what you call old Adam's Fall,
    and only his Trespass,
You call amiss to call it his,
    both his and yours it was.

172

He was design'd of all Mankind
    to be a publick Head,
A common Root, whence all should shoot,
    and stood in all their stead.
He stood and fell, did ill or well,   *1 Cor. 15:48, 49.*
    not for himself alone,
But for you all, who now his Fall,
    and trespass would disown.

173

If he had stood, then all his brood
    had been established
In Gods true love, never to move,
    nor once awry to tread:
Then all his Race, my Father's Grace,
    should have enjoy'd for ever,
And wicked Sprights by subtile sleights
    could them have harmed never.

174

Would you have griev'd to have receiv'd
    through *Adam* so much good,
As had been your for evermore,
    if he at first had stood?
Would you have said, we ne'r obey'd,
    nor did thy Laws regard;
It ill befits with benefits,
    us, Lord, so to reward?

175

Since then to share in his welfare,
    you could have been content,
You may with reason share in his treason,
    and in the punishment.
Hence you were born in state forlorn,   *Rom. 5:12.*
    with Natures so depraved: *Ps. 51:5.*
Death was your due, because that you   *Gen. 5:3.*
    had thus your selves behaved.

176

You think if we had been as he,
    whom God did so betrust,
We to our cost would ne're have lost
    all for a paltry Lust.
Had you been made in *Adam's* stead,
    you would like things have wrought,
And so into the self-same wo,
    your selves and yours have brought.

Matt. 23:30, 31.

177

I may deny you once to try,
    or Grace to you to tender,
Though he finds Grace before my face,
    who was the chief offender:
Else should my Grace cease to be Grace;
    for it should not be free,
If to release whom I should please,
    I have no libertee.

Rom. 9:15, 18.
The free gift.
Rom. 5:15.

178

If upon one what's due to none
    I frankly shall bestow,
And on the rest shall not think best,
    compassions skirts to throw,
Whom injure I? will you envy,
    and grudge at others weal?
Or me accuse, who do refuse
    your selves to help and heal?

179

Am I alone of what's my own,
    no Master or no Lord?
Or if I am, how can you claim
    what I to some afford?
Will you demand Grace at my hand,
    and challenge what is mine?
Will you teach me whom to set free,
    & thus my Grace confine?

Matt. 20:15.

180

You sinners are, and such a share
    as sinners may expect,
Such you shall have; for I do save
    none but mine own Elect.
Yet to compare your sin with their,
    who liv'd a longer time,
I do confess yours is much less,
    though every sin's a crime.

Ps. 58:3.
Rom. 6:23.
Gal. 3:10.
Rom. 8:29, 30; 11:7.
Rev. 21:27.
Luke 12:48.

181

A crime it is, therefore in bliss
    you may not hope to dwell;
But unto you I shall allow
    the easiest room in Hell.
The glorious King thus answering,
    they cease, and plead no longer:
Their Consciences must needs confess
    his Reasons are the stronger.

Matt. 11:22.
The wicked all
convinced and put to
silence.
Rom. 3:19.
Matt. 22:12.

182

Thus all mens Pleas the Judge with ease
    doth answer and confute,
Until that all, both great and small,
    are silenced and mute.
Vain hopes are cropt, all mouths are stopt,
    sinners have nought to say,
But that 'tis just, and equal most
    they should be damn'd for ay.

Behold the formidable
estate of all the
ungodly, as they stand
hopeless & helpless
before an impartial
Judge, expecting their
final Sentence.
Rev. 6:16, 17.

183

Now what remains, but that to pains
    and everlasting smart,
Christ should condemn the Sons of men,
    which is their just desert;
Oh, rueful plights of sinful wights!
    Oh wretches all forlorn!
'T had happy been they ne're had seen
    the Sun, or not been born.

184

Yea, now it would be good they could
    themselves annihilate,
And cease to be, themselves to free
    from such a fearful state.
Oh happy Dogs, and Swine, and Frogs:
    yea Serpents generation,
Who do not fear this doom to hear,
    and sentence of Damnation!

185

This is their state so desperate: *Ps. 139:2, 3, 4.*
    their sins are fully known;   *Eccles. 12:14.*
Their vanities and villanies
    before the world are shown.
As they are gross and impious,
    so are their numbers more
Than motes i' th' Air, or then their hair,
    or sands upon the shore.

186

Divine Justice offended is
    and Satisfaction claimeth:
God's wrathful ire kindled like fire,
    against them fiercely flameth.
Their Judge severe doth quite cashier
    and all their Pleas off take,   *Matt. 25:45.*
That never a man, or dare, or can
    a further Answer make.

187

Their mouths are shut, each man is put   *Matt. 22:12.*
    to silence and to shame: *Rom. 2:5, 6.*
Nor have they ought within their thought,   *Luke 19:42.*
    Christ's Justice for to blame.
The Judge is just, and plague them must,
    nor will he mercy shew
(For Mercies day is past away)
    to any of this Crew.

188

The Judge is strong, doers of wrong
    cannot his power withstand:
None can by flight run out of sight,
    nor scape out of his hand.
Sad is their state: for Advocate
    to plead their Cause there's none:
None to prevent their punishment,
    or misery bemone.

Matt. 28:18.
Ps. 139:7.

189

O dismal day! wither shall they
    for help and succour flee?
To God above, with hopes to move
    their grestest Enemee:
His wrath is great, whose burning heat
    no floods of tears can slake:
His word stands fast, that they be cast
    into the burning Lake.

Isa. 33:14.
Ps. 11:6.
Num. 23:19.

190

To Christ their Judge, he doth adjudge
    them to the Pit of Sorrow;
Nor will he hear, or cry, or tear,
    nor respite them one morrow.
To Heav'n alas, they cannot pass,
    it is against them shut;
To enter there [O heavy cheer]
    they out of hopes are put.

Matt. 25:41.

Matt. 25:10, 11, 12.

191

Unto their Treasures, or to their Pleasures,
    all these have them forsaken:
Had they full Coffers to make large offers,
    their Gold would not be taken
Unto the place where whilome was
    their Birth and Education?
Lo! Christ begins for their great sins
    to fire the Earths Foundation:

Luke 12:20.
Ps. 49:7, 17.

Deut. 32:22.

192

And by and by the flaming Sky	*2 Pet. 3:10.*
shall drop like molten Lead	

And by and by the flaming Sky
    shall drop like molten Lead
About their ears, t' increase their fears,
    and aggravate their dread.
To Angels good that ever stood
    in their integrity,
Should they betake themselves, and make
    their sute incessantly?

2 Pet. 3:10.

193

They neither skill, nor do they will
    to work them any ease:
They will not mourn to see them burn,
    nor beg for their release.
To wicked men, their bretheren
    in sin and wickedness,
Should they make mone? their case is one,
    they're in the same distress.

Matt. 13:41, 42.

Rev. 20:13, 15.

194

Ah, cold comfort, and mean support
    from such like Comforters!
Ah, little joy of Company,
    and fellow-sufferers!
Such shall increase their hearts disease,
    and add unto their woe,
Because that they brought to decay
    themselves and many moe.

Luke 16:28.

195

Unto the Saints with sad complaints
    should they themselves apply?
They're not dejected, nor ought affected
    with all their misery.
Friends stand aloof, and make no proof
    what Prayers or Tears can do:
Your godly friends are now more friends
    to Christ than unto you.

Rev. 21:4.

Ps. 58:10.

196

Where tender love mens hearts did move
    unto a sympathy,
And bearing part of others smart
    in their anxiety;
Now such compassion is out of fashion,
    and wholly laid aside:
No Friends so near, but Saints to hear
    their Sentence can abide.

1 Cor. 6:2.

197

One natural Brother beholds another
    in this astonied fit,
Yet sorrows not thereat a jot,
    nor pitties him a whit.
The godly wife conceives no grief,
    nor can she shed a tear
For the sad state of her dear Mate,
    when she his doom doth hear.

Compare
Prov. 1:26 with
1 John 3:2 &
2 Cor. 5:16.

198

He that was erst a Husband pierc't
    with sense of Wives distress,
Whose tender heart did bear a part
    of all her grievances,
Shall mourn no more as heretofore
    because of her ill plight
Although he see her now to be
    a damn'd forsaken wight.

199

The tender Mother will own no other
    of all her numerous brood,
But such as stand at Christ's right hand
    acquitted through his Blood.
The pious Father had now much rather
    his graceless Son should ly
In Hell with Devils, for all his evils
    burning eternally,

Luke 16:25.

200

Then God most high should injury,
    by sparing him sustain;
And doth rejoyce to hear Christ's voice
    adjudging him to pain;
Who having all, both great and small,
    convinc'd and silenced,
Did then proceed their Doom to read,
    and thus it uttered:

Ps. 58:10.

201

Ye sinful wights, and cursed sprights,
    that work Iniquity,
Depart together from me for ever
    to endless Misery;
Your portion take in yonder Lake,
    where Fire and Brimstone flameth:
Suffer the smart, which your desert
    as it's due wages claimeth.

*The Judge
pronounceth the
sentence of
condemnation.
Matt. 25:41.*

202

Oh piercing words more sharp than swords!
    what, to depart from Thee,
Whose face before for evermore
    the best of Pleasures be!
What? to depart (unto our smart)
    from thee *Eternally*:
To be for aye banish'd away,
    with *Devils* company!

The terrour of it.

203

What? to be sent to *Punishment,*
    and flames of *Burning Fire,*
To be surrounded, and eke confounded
    with Gods *Revengful ire.*
What? to abide, not for a tide
    these Torments, but for *Ever*:
To be released, or to be eased,
    not after years, but *Never.*

204

Oh, *fearful Doom!* now there's no room
    for hope or help at all:
Sentence is past which aye shall last,
    Christ will not it recall.
There might you hear them rent and tear
    the Air with their out-cries:
The hideous noise of their sad voice
    ascendeth to the Skies.

205

They wring their hands, their caitiff-hands   *Luke 13:28.*
    and gnash their teeth for terrour;
They cry, they roar for anguish sore,
    and gnaw their tongues for horrour.
But get away without delay,
    Christ pitties not your cry:
Depart to Hell, there may you yell,
    and roar Eternally.   *Prov. 1:26.*

206

That word, *Depart*, maugre their heart,   *It is put in Execution.*
    drives every wicked one,
With mighty pow'r, the self-same hour,
    far from the Judge's Throne.
Away they're chaste by the strong blast   *Matt. 25:46.*
    of his Death-threatning mouth:
They flee full fast, as if in haste,
    although they be full loath.

207

As chaff that's dry, and dust doth fly
    before the Northern wind:
Right so are they chased away,
    and can no Refuge find.
They hasten to the Pit of Wo,
    guarded by Angels stout;   *Matt. 13:41, 42.*
Who to fulfil Christ's holy will,
    attend this wicked Rout.

208

Whom having brought, as they are taught,
    unto the brink of Hell
(That dismal place far from Christ's face,
    where Death and Darkness dwell:
Where Gods fierce Ire kindleth the fire,
    and vengeance feeds the flame
With piles of Wood, and Brimstone Flood,
    that none can quench the same,)

HELL.
Matt. 25:30.
Mark 9:43.
Isa. 30:33.
Rev. 21:8.

209

With Iron bands they bind their hands,
    and cursed feet together,
And cast them all, both great and small,
    into that Lake for ever.
Where day and night, without respite,
    they wail, and cry, and howl
For tort'ring pain, which they sustain
    in Body and in Soul.

Wicked Men and Devils
cast into it for ever.
Matt. 22:13; 25:46.

210

For day and night, in their despight,
    their torments smoak ascendeth.
Their pain and grief have no relief,
    their anguish never endeth.
There must they ly, and never dy,
    though dying every day:
There must they dying ever ly,
    and not consume away.

Rev. 14:10.

211

Dy fain they would, if dy they could,
    but Death will not be had.
God's direful wrath their bodies hath
    for ev'r Immortal made.
They live to ly in misery,
    and bear eternal wo;
And live they must whilst God is just,
    that he may plague them so.

212

But who can tell the plagues of Hell,
    and torments exquisite?
Who can relate their dismal state,
    and terrours infinite?
Who fare the best, and feel the least,
    yet feel that punishment
Whereby to nought they should be brought,
    if God did not prevent.

The unsufferable
torments of the
damned.
Luke 16:24.
Jude 7.

213

The least degree of miserie
    there felt's incomparable,
The lightest pain they there sustain
    more than intolerable.
But God's great pow'r from hour to hour
    upholds them in the fire,
That they shall not consume a jot,
    nor by it's force expire.

Isa. 33:14.
Mark 9:43, 44.

214

But ah, the wo they undergo
    (they more than all besides)
Who has the light, and knew the right,
    yet would not it abide.
The sev'n-fold smart, which to their part,
    and portion doth fall,
Who Christ his Grace would not imbrace,
    nor hearken to his call.

Luke 12:47.

215

The *Amorites* and *Sodomites*
    although their plagues be sore,
Yet find some ease, compar'd to these,
    who feel a great deal more.
Almighty God, whose Iron Rod,
    to smite them never lins,
Doth most declare his Justice rare
    in plaguing these mens sins.

Matt. 11:24.

216

The pain of loss their Souls doth toss,
    and wond'rously distress,
To think what they have cast away
    by wilful wickedness.
We might have been redeem'd from sin
    think they, and liv'd above,
Being possest of heav'nly rest,
    and joying in God's love.

Luke 16:23, 25.
Luke 13:28.

217

But wo, wo, wo our Souls into!
    we would not happy be;
And therefore bear Gods Vengeance here
    to all Eternitee.
Experience and woful sense
    must be our painful teachers
Who n'ould believe, nor credit give,
    unto our faithful Preachers.

Luke 13:34.

218

Thus shall they ly, and wail, and cry,
    tormented, and tormenting
Their galled hearts with pois'ned darts
    but now too late repenting
There let them dwell i' th' Flames of Hel
    there leave we them to burn,
And back agen unto the men
    whom Christ acquits, return.

Mark 9:44.
Rom. 2:15.

219

The Saints behold with courage bold,
    and thankful wonderment,
To see all those that were their foes
    thus sent to punishment:
Then do they sing unto their King
    a Song of endless Praise:
They praise his Name, and do proclaim
    that just are all his ways.

The Saints rejoyce to
see Judgement executed
upon the wicked World.
Ps. 58:10.
Rev. 19:1, 2, 3.

220

Thus with great joy and melody
 to Heav'n they all ascend,
Him there to praise with sweetest layes,
 and Hymns that never end.
Where with long Rest they shall be blest,
 and nought shall them annoy:
Where they shall see as seen they be,
 and whom they love enjoy.

*They ascend with Christ
into Heaven
triumphing.
Matt. 25:46.
1 John 3:2.
1 Cor. 13:12.*

221

O glorious Place! where face to face
 Jehovah may be seen,
By such as were sinners whilere
 and no dark vail between.
Where the Sun shine, and light Divine,
 of Gods bright Countenance,
Doth rest upon them every one.
 with sweetest influence.

*Their Eternal hapiness
and incomparable
Glory there.*

222

O blessed state of the Renate!
 O wondrous Happiness,
To which they're brought, beyond what thought
 can reach, or words express!
Griefs water-course, and sorrows sourse,
 are turn'd to joyful streams,
Their old distress and heaviness
 are vanished like dreams.

Rev. 21:4.

223

For God above in arms of love
 doth dearly them embrace,
And fills their sprights with such delights,
 and pleasures in his grace;
As shall not fail, nor yet grow stale
 through frequency of use:
Nor do they fear Gods favour there,
 to forfeit by abuse.

Ps. 16:11.

224

For there the Saints are perfect Saints,   *Heb. 12:23.*
   and holy ones indeed,
From all the sin that dwelt within
   their mortal bodies freed:
Made Kings and Priests to God through Christs
   dear loves transcendency,   *Rev. 1:6; 22:5.*
There to remain, and there to reign
   with him Eternally.

FINIS.

A Short Discourse on Eternity

1

What Mortal man can with his Span
    mete out Eternity?
Or fathom it by depth of Wit,
    or strength of Memory?
The lofty Sky is not so high,
    Hells depth to this is small:
The World so wide is but a stride,
    compared therewithall.

Isa. 57:15.
Mark 3:29.
Matt. 25:46.

2

It is a main great Ocean,
    withouten bank or bound:
A deep Abyss, wherein there is
    no bottom to be found.
This World hath stood now since the Flood,
    four thousand years well near,
And hath before endured more
    than sixteen hundred year.

3

But what's the time from the Worlds prime
    unto this present day,
If we thereby Eternity
    to measure should assay?
The whole duration since the Creation
    though long, yet is more little,
If placed by Eternity,
    then is the smallest tittle.

4

Tell every Star both near and far,
    in Heav'ns bright Canopee,
That doth appear throughout the year,
    of high or low degree:
Tell every Tree that thou canst see
    in this vast Wilderness,
Up in the Woods, down by the Floods,
    in thousand miles progress.

5

The sum is bast, yet not so vast,
    but that thou may'st go on
To multiply the Leaves thereby,
    that hang those Trees upon:
And thereunto the Drops, that thou
    imaginest to be
In April Show'rs, that bring forth Flow'rs,
    and blossoms plenteously:

6

Number the Fowls and living Souls
    that through the Air do Fly,
The winged Hosts in all their Coasts
    beneath the Starry Sky:
Count all the Grass as thou doast pass
    through many a pasture-land,
And dewy Drops that on the tops
    of Herbs and Plants do stand.

7

Number the Sand upon the Strand,
    and Atomes of the Air;
And do thy best on Man and Beast,
    to reckon every Hair:
Take all the Dust, if so thou lust,   *2 Thess. 1:9.*
    and add to thine Account: *Rev. 14:11.*
Yet shall the Years of sinners tears,
    the Number far surmount.

8

Nought joyn'd to nought can ne're make ought,
    nor Cyphers make a Sum:
Nor things Finite, to infinite
    by multiplying come:
A Cockle-shell may serve as well
    to lade the Ocean dry,
As finite things and Reckonings
    to bound Eternity.

9

O happy they that live for aye,
    with Christ in Heav'n above!   *1 Thess. 4:17.*
Who know withal, that nothing shall   *Rom. 8:38, 39.*
    deprive them of his love.
Eternity, Eternity!
    Oh, were it not for thee,
The Saints in bliss and happiness
    could never happy be.

10

For if they were in any fear,
    that this their joy might cease,   *1 John 4:18.*
It would annoy [if not destroy]   *John 6:35, 40, 51.*
    and interrupt their peace: *Rev. 21:4.*
But being sure it shall endure
    so long as God shall live;
The thoughts of this unto their bliss,
    do full perfection give.

11

Cheer up, ye Saints, amidst your wants,   *Heb. 12:12.*
    and sorrows many a one.
Lift up the head, shake off all dread,
    and moderate your mone.
Your sufferings and evil things
    will suddenly be past;   *2 Cor. 4:17.*
Your sweet Fruitions, and blessed Visions,   *Ps. 16:11.*
    for evermore shall last.

12

Lament and mourn you that must burn
    amidst those flaming Seas:
If once you come to such a doom,
    for ever farewel ease.
O sad estate and desperate,
    that never can be mended,
Until Gods Will shall change, or til
    Eternity be ended!

Luke 13:28.
Matt. 25:41, 46.
Rev. 14:11.

13

If any one this Question
    shall unto me propound;
What, have the years of sinners tears
    no limits, or no bound?
It kills our heart to think of smart,
    and pains that last for ever;
And hear of fire that shall expire,
    or be extinguish'd never.

Mark 9:43, 44.

14

I'le Answer make (or let them take
    my words as I intend them:
For this is all the Cordial
    that here I have to lend them)
When Heav'n shall cease to flow with peace
    and all felicity;
Then Hell may cease to be the place
    of Wo and Misery.

15

When Heav'n is Hell, when Ill is Well,
    when Vertue turns to Vice,
When wrong is Right, and Dark is Light,
    when Nought is of great price:
Then may the years of sinners tears
    and surferings expire,
And all the hosts of damned ghosts
    escape out of Hell-fire.

16

When Christ above shall cease to love,
    when God shall cease to reign,
And be no more, as heretofore,
    the Worlds great Sovereign.
Or not be just, or favour lust,
    or in mens sins delight:
Then wicked men [and not till then]
    to Heav'n may take their flight.

17

When Gods great Power shall be brought lower,
    by forreign Puissance;
Or be decay'd, and weaker made
    through Times continuance:
When drowsiness shall him oppress,
    and lay him fast asleep:
Then sinful men may break their pen,
    and out of Prison creep.

18

When those in Glory shall be right sory
    they may not change their place,
And wish to dwell with them in Hell,
    never to see Christs face:
Then those in pain may freedom gain,
    and be with Glory dight:
Then Hellish Fiends may be Christs Friends,
    and Heirs of Heaven hight.

19

Then, Ah poor men! what, not till then?
    No, not an hour before:
For God is just, and therefore must
    torment them evermore.
ETERNITY! ETERNITY!
    thou mak'st hard hearts to bleed:
The thoughts of thee in misery,
    do make men wail indeed.

20

When they remind what's still behind,
    and ponder this word NEVER,
That they must here be made to bear   *Mark 9:43, 44, 45, 46,*
    Gods Vengeance for EVER: *&c.*
The thought of this more bitter is,
    then all they feel beside:
Yet what they feel, nor heart of steel,
    nor Flesh of Brass can bide.

21

To lye in wo, and undergo
    the direful pains of Hell,
And know withall, that there they shall   *2 Thess. 1:8, 9.*
    for aye, and ever dwell;
And that they are from rest as far
    when fifty thousand year,   *Matt. 25:46.*
Twice told, are spent in punishment,   *Rev. 14:10, 11.*
    as when they first came there.

22

This, Oh! this makes Hells fiery flakes
    much more intolerable;
This makes frail wights & damned sprights,
    to bear their plagues unable.
This makes men bite, for fell despite,
    their very tongues in twain:
This makes them rore for great horror,
    and trebleth all their pain.

A Postscript unto the Reader

And now good Reader, I return again
To talk with thee, who has been at the pain
To read throughout, & heed what went before;
And unto thee I'le speak a little more.
Give ear, I pray to thee, unto what I say,   5
That God may hear thy voice another day.
Thou hast a Soul, my friend, and so have I,
To save or lose; a Soul that cannot die,
A soul of greater price than Gold or Gems;
A Soul more worth than Crowns and Diadems;   10
A Soul at first created like its Maker,
And of Gods Image made to be partaker:
Upon the wings of Noblest Faculties,
Taught for to soar above the Starry Skies,
And not to rest, until it understood   15
It self possessed of the chiefest good.
And since the Fall thy Soul retaineth still
Those Faculties of Reason and of Will,
But Oh, how much deprav'd, and out of frame,
As if they were some others, not the same.   20
Thine Understanding dismally benighted,
And Reason's eye in Sp'ritual things dim-sighted,
Or else stark blind: Thy Will inclin'd to evil,
And nothing else, a Slave unto the Devil;
That loves to live, and liveth to transgress,   25
But shuns the way of God and Holiness.
All thine Affections are disordered;
And thou by head-strong Passions are misled.
What need I tell thee of the crooked way,
And many wicked wand'rings every day?   30
Or that think own transgressions are more
In number, than the sands upon the Shore:
Thou are a lump of wickedness become,
And may'st with horrour think upon they Doom.
Until thy Soul be washed in the flood   35

Of Christ's most dear, soul-cleansing precious blood.
That, that alone can do away thy sin
Which thou wert born, and hast long lived in,
That, only that, can pacifie Gods wrath,
If apprehended by a lively Faith,   40
Now whilst the day and means of Grace to last,
Before the opportunity be past.
But if, O man, thou liv'st a Christless creature,
And Death surprize thee in a state of nature,
(As who can tell but that may be thy case)   45
How wilt thou stand before the Judge's face?
When he shall be reveal'd in flaming fire,
And come to pay ungodly men their hire:
To execute due vengeance upon those
That knew him not, or that have been his foes?   50
What wilt thou answer unto his demands,
When he requires a reason at thy hands
Of all the things that thou has said, or done,
Or left undone, or set thine heart upon?
When he shall thus with thee expostulate,   55
What cause hadst thou thy Maker for to hate,
To take up Arms against thy Soveraign,
And Emnity against him to maintain?
What injury hath God Almighty done thee?
What good hath he with-held that might have won thee?   60
What evil, or injustice, hast thou found
In him, that might unto thine hurt redound?
If neither felt, nor feared injury
Hath moved thee to such hostility,
What made thee then the Fountain to forsake,   65
And unto broken Pits thy self betake?
What reason hadst thou to dishonour God,
Who thee with Mercies never cease to load?
Because the Lord was good, hast thou been evil,
And taken part against him with the Devil?   70
For all his cost to pay him with despite,
And all his love with hatred to requite?
Is this the fruit of Gods great patience,
To wax more bold in disobedience?
To kick against the bowels of his Love,   75
Is this aright his Bounty to improve?
Stand still, ye Heav'ns and be astonished,
That God by man should thus be injured!

Give ear, O earth, and tremble at the sin
Of those that thine Inhabitants have bin.   80
But thou, vile wretch, hast added unto all
Thine other faults, and facts so criminal,
The damning sin of wilful unbelief,
Of all Transgressors hadst thou been the chief;
Yet when time was, thou might'st have been set free   85
From Sin, and Wrath, and punishment by mee.
But thou wouldst not accept of Gospel Grace,
Nor on my terms Eternal Life embrace.
As if that all thy breaches of Gods Law
Were not enough upon thy head to draw   90
Eternal Wrath: Thou hast despis'd a Saviour,
Rejected me, and trampled on my favour.
How oft have I stood knocking at thy door,
And been denied entrance evermore?
How often hath my Spirit been withstood,   95
When as I sent him to have done thee good?
Thou hast no need of nay one to plead
Thy Cause, or for thy Soul to intercede:
Plead for thy self, if thou has ought to say,
And pay thy forfeiture without delay.   100
Behold thou dost ten thousand Talents owe,
Or pay thy Debt, or else to Prison go.
Think, think, O Man, when Christ shall thus unfold
Thy secret guilt, and make thee to behold
The ugly face of all thy sinful errours,   105
And fill thy Soul with his amazing terrours,
And let thee see the flaming Pit of Hell
(Where all that have no part in him shall dwell)
When he shall thus expostulate the case,
How canst thou bear to look him in the face?   110
What wilt thou do without an Advocate?
Or plead, when as thy state is desperate?
Dost think to put him off with fair pretences?
Or wilt thou hide and cover thine offences?
Can any think from him concealed be,   115
Who doth the hidden things of darkness see?
Art thou of force his Power to withstand?
Canst thou by might escape out of his hand?
Dost thou intend to run out of his sight,
And save thy self from punishment by flight?   120
Or wilt thou be eternally accurst,

And bide his Vengeance, let him do his worst?
Oh, who can bear his indignations heat?
Or bide the pains of Hell, which are so great?
If then thou neither canst his Wrath endure,   125
Nor any Ransom after death procure:
If neither Cryes nor Tears can move his heart
To pardon thee, or mittigate thy smart,
But unto Hell thou must perforce be sent
With dismal horrour and astonishment: 130
Consider, O my Friends, what cause thou hast
With fear and trembling (while as yet thou mayst)
To lay to heart thy sin and misery,
And to make out after the Remedy.
Consider well the greatness of my danger,   135
O Child of wrath, and object of Gods anger.
Thou hangest over the Infernal Pit
By one small threed, and car'st thou not a whit?
There's but a step between thy Soul and Death,
Nothing remains but stopping of thy breath,   140
(Which may be done to morrow, or before)
And then thou art undone for evermore.
Let this awaken thy Security,
And make thee look about thee speedily,
How canst thou rest an hour or sleep a night,   145
Or in thy Creature-comforts take delight;
Or with vain Toyes thy self forgetfull make
How near thou art unto the burning Lake?
How canst thou live without tormenting fears?
How canst thou hold from weeping floods of tears,   150
Yea, tears of blood, I might almost have sed,
If such like tears could from thine eyes be shed?
To gain the world what will it prorlt thee,
And loose thy Soul and self eternallie?
Eternity on one small point dependeth: 155
The man is lost that this short life mispendeth,
For as the Tree doth fall, right so it lies;
And man continues in what state he dies.
Who happy die, shall happy rise again;
Who cursed die, shall cursed still remain,   160
If under Sin, and Wrath, Death leaves thee bound,
At Judgment under Wrath thou shalt be found:
And then wo, wo that ever thou wert born,
O wretched man, of Heav'n and Earth forlorn!

Consider this, all ye that God forget,   165
Who all his threatenings at nought do set,
Lest into pieces he begin to tear
Your Souls, and there be no deliverer.
O you that now sing care and fear away,
Think often of the formidable Day,   170
Wherein the Heavens with a mighy noise,
And with a hideous, heart-confounding voice,
Shall pass away together, being roll'd
As men are wont their garments for to fold.
When th' Elements with fervent heat shall melt,   175
And living Creatures in the same shall swelt,
And altogether in those Flames expire,
Which set the Earths Foundations on fire.
Oh, what amazement will your hearts be in,
And how will you to curse your selves begin   180
For all your damned sloth, and negligence,
And unbelief, and gross Impenitence,
When you shall hear that dreadful Sentence past,
That all the wicked into Hell be cast?
What horrour will your Consciences surprise,   185
When you shall hear the fruitless doleful cries
Of such as are compelled to depart
Unto the place of everlasting smart?
What, when you see the sparks fly out of Hell,
And view the Dungeon where you are to dwell,   190
Wherein you must eternally remain
In anguish, and intolerable pain?
What, when your hands & feet are bound together,
And you are cast into that Lake for ever?
Then shall you feel the truth of what you hear,   195
That hellish pains are more than you can bear,
And that those Torments are an hundred fold
More terrible than ever you were told,
Nor speak I this, good Reader, to torment thee
Beforc the time, but rather to prevent thee   200
From running head-long to thine own decay,
In such a perillous and deadly way
We, who have known and felt Jehovah's terrours,
Perswade men to repent them of their errours,
And turn to God in time, e're his Decree   205
Bring forth, and then there be no Remedee!
If in the night, when thou art fast asleep,

Some friend of thine, that better watch doth keep,
Should see thy house all on a burning flame,
And thee almost inclosed with the same: 210
If such a friend should break thy door & wake thee,
Or else by force out of the peril take thee:
What? wouldst thou take his kindness in ill part?
Or frown upon him for his good desert?
Such, O my friend, such is thy present state,   215
And danger, being unregenerate.
Awake, awake, and then thou shalt perceive
Thy peril greater then thou wilt believe.
Lift up thine eyes, and see Gods wrathful ire,
preparing unextinguishable fire   220
For all that live and die impenitent.
Awake, awake, O Sinner, and repent,
And quarrel not, because I thus alarm
Thy Soul to save it from eternal harm.
Perhaps thou harbourest such thoughts as these: 225
I hope I may enjoy my carnal ease
A little longer, and my self refresh
With those delights that gratifie the flesh;
And yet repent before it be too late,
And get into a comfortable state   230
I hope I have yet many years to spend,
And time enough those matters to attend.
Presumptuous heart! Is God engag'd to give
A longer time to such as love to live
Like Rebels still, who think to stain his Glory   235
By wickedness, and after to be sory?
Unto thy lust shall he be made a drudge,
Who thee, and all ungodly men, shall judge?
Canst thou account sin sweet, and yet confess,
That first, or last, it ends in bitterness?   240
Is sin a thing that must procure thee sorrow?
And wouldst thou dally with't another morrow?
O foolish man, who lovest to enjoy
That which will thee distress, or else destroy!
What gained Sampson by his Delilah?   245
What gained David by his Bathsheba?
The one became a Slave, lost both his eyes,
And made them sport that were his Enemies:
The other penneth, as a certain token
Of Gods displeasure, that his bones were broken,   250

Besides the woes he after met withal,
To chasten him for that his grievous Fall:
His own Son Ammon using crafy wiles,
His Daughter Thamar wickedly defiles;
His second Son more beautiful than good,   255
His hands embreweth in his Brothers Blood:
And by and by aspiring to the Crown,
He strives to pull his gentle Father down:
With hellish rage, him fiercely persecuting,
And bruitishly his concubines polluting.   260
Read whoso list, and ponder what he reads,
And he shall find small joy in evil deeds.
Moreover this consider, that the longer
Thou liv'st in sin, thy sin will grow the stronger.
And then it will an harder matter prove,   265
To leave those wicked haunts that thou dost love.
The Black-moor may as eas'ly change his skin,
As old transgressors leave their wonted sin.
And who can tell what may become of thee,
Or where thy Soul in one days time may be?   270
We see that Death ner old nor young men spares,
But one and other takes at unawares.
For in a moment, whil'st men Peace do cry,
Destruction seizeth on them suddenly.
Thou who this morning art a lively wight,   275
May'st be a Crops and damned Ghost ere night.
Oh, dream not then, that it will serve the turn,
Upon thy death bed for thy sins to mourn.
But think how many have been snatcht away,
And had no time for mercy once to pray.   280
It's just with God Repentance to deny
To such as put it off until they dy.
And late Repentance seldom proveth true,
Which if it fail, thou know'st what must ensue.
For after this short life is at an end,   285
What is amiss thou never canst amend.
Believe, O man, that to procrastinate,
And put it off until it be too late,
As 'tis thy sin, so is it Satans wile,
Whereby he doth great multitudes beguile.   290
How many thousands hath this strong delusion
Already brought to ruine and confusion,
Whose Souls are now reserv'd in Iron Chains,

Under thick darkness to eternal pains?
They thought of many years, as thou dost now,   295
But were deceived quite, and so may'st thou.
Oh, then my friend, while not away thy time,
Nor by rebellion aggravate thy Crime.
Oh put not off Repentance till to morrow,
Adventure not without Gods leave to borrow   300
Another day to spend upon thy lust,
Lest God (that is most holy, wise, and just)
Denounce in wrath, and to thy terrour say
This night shall Devils fetch thy Soul away.
Now seek the face of God with all thy heart;   305
Acknowledge unto him how vile thou art.
Tell him thy sins deserve eternal wrath,
And that it is a wonder that he hath
Permitted thee so long to draw thy breath,
Who might have cut thee off by sudden death,   310
And sent thy Soul into the lowest Pit,
From whence no price should ever ransom it,
And that he may most justly do it still
(Because thou hast deserv'd it) if he will.
Yet also tell him that, if he shall please,   315
He can forgive thy Sins, and thee release.
And that in Christ his Son he may be just,
And justifie all those that on him trust:
That though thy sins are of a crimson dy,
Yet Christ his Blood can cleanse thee thorowly.   320
Tell him, that he may make his glorious Name
More wonderful by covering thy shame.
That Mercy may be greatly magnify'd,
And Justice also fully satisfy'd,
If he shall please to own thee in his Son,   325
Who hath paid dear for Men's Redemption.
Tell him thou hast an unbelieving heart,
Which hindereth thee from coming for a part
In Christ: and that although his terrours aw thee,
Thou canst not come till he be pleas'd to draw thee.   330
Tell him thou know'st thine heart to be so bad,
And thy condition so exceeding sad,
That though Salvation may be had for nought,
Thou canst not come and take, till thou be brought.
Oh beg of him to bow thy stubborn Will   335
To come to Christ, that he thy lusts may kill.

Look up to Christ for his attractive pow'r,
Which he exerteth in a needful hour;
Who saith, whenas I lifted up shall be,
Then will I draw all sorts of men to me.   340
O wait upon him with true diligence,
And trembling fear in every Ordinance.
Unto his call earnest attention give,
Whose voice makes deaf men hear, and dead men live.
Thus weep, and mourn, thus hearken, pray and wait,   345
Till he behold, and pitty thine estate,
Who is more ready to bestow his Grace,
Then thou the same art willing to imbrace;
Yea, he hath Might enough to bring thee home,
Though thou hast neither strength nor will to come.   350
If he delay to answer thy request,
Know that oft-times he doth it fot the best,
Not with intent to drive us from his door,
But for to make us importune him more;
Or else to bring us duly to confess,   355
And be convinc'd of our unworthiness.
Oh, be not weary then, but persevere
To beg his Grace till he thy suit shall hear:
And leave him not, nor from his foot-stool go,
Till over thee Compassions skirt he throw.   360
Eternal Life will recompence thy pains,
If found at last, with everlasting gains.
For if the Lord be pleas'd to hear thy cryes,
And to forgive thy great iniquities;
Thou wilt have cause for ever to admire,   365
And laud his Grace, that granted thy desire.
Then shalt thou find thy labour is not lost:
But that the good obtain'd surmounts the cost.
Nor shall thou grieve for loss of sinful pleasures,
Exchang'd for heavenly joyes and lasting treasures.   370
The yoke of Christ, which once thou didst esteem
A tedious yoke, shall then most easie seem.
For why? The love of Christ shall thee constrain
To take delight in that which was thy pain.
The wayes of Wisdom shall be pleasant wayes,   375
And thou shalt chuse therein to spend thy dayes;
If once thy Soul be brought to such a pass:
O'bless the Lord, and magnifie his Grace.
Thou, that of late hadst reason to be sad,

May'st now rejoyce, and be excceeding glad,   380
For thy condition is as happy now,
As erst it was disconsolate and low.
Thou art become as rich as whilome poor,
As blessed now, as cursed heretofore.
For being cleansed with Christs precious Blood,   385
Thou hast an int'rest in the chiefest good:
Gods anger is towards thy Soul appeased,
And in his Christ he is with thee well pleased.
Yea, he doth look upon thee with a mild
And gracious aspect as upon his child.   390
He is become thy Father and thy Friend,
And will defend thee from the cursed Fiend.
Thou need'st not fear the roaring Lyon's rage,
Since God Almighty doth himself engage
To bear thy Soul in Everlasting Armes,   395
Above the reach of all destructive harms.
What ever here thy sufferings may be,
Yet from them all the Lord shall rescue thee.
He will preserve thee by his wond'rous might
Unto that rich Inheritance in light.   400
Oh, sing for joy, all ye regenerate,
Whom Christ hath brought into this blessed state!
O love the Lord, all ye his Saints, who hath
Redeemed you from everlasting wrath:
Who hath by dying made your Souls to live,   405
And what he dearly bought doth freely give:
Give up your selves to walk in all his wayes,
And study how to live unto his praise.
The time is short you have to serve him here:
The day of your deliv'rance draweth near.   410
Lift up your heads, ye upright ones in heart,
Who in Christ's purchase have obtain'd a part.
Behold, he rides upon a shining Cloud,
With Angels voice, and Trumpet sounding loud;
He comes to save his folk from all their foes,   415
And plague the men that Holiness oppose.
So come, Lord Jesus, quickly come we pray
Yea come, and hasten our Redemption day.

A Song of Emptiness

To Fill up the Empty Pages Following

Vanity of Vanities

Vain, frail, short liv'd, and miserable Man,
Learn what thou art when thine estate is best:
A restless Wave o'th' troubled Ocean,
A Dream, a lifeless Picture finely drest:

A Wind, a Flower, a Vapour, and a Bubble,   5
A Wheel that stands not still, a trembling Reed,
A rolling Stone, dry Dust, light Chaff, and Stubble,
A Shadow of Something, but nought indeed.

Learn what deceitful Toyes, and empty things,
This World, and all its best Enjoyments bee: 10
Out of the Earth no true Contentment springs,
But all things here are vexing Vanitee.

For what is *Beauty*, but a fading Flower?
Or what is *Pleasure*, but the Devils bait,
Whereby he catcheth whom he would devour,   15
And multitudes of Souls doth ruinate?

And what are *Friends* but mortal men, as we?
Whom Death from us may quickly separate;
Or else their hearts may quite estranged be,
And all their love be turned into hate.   20

And what are *Riches* to be doted on?
Uncertain, fickle, and ensnaring things;
They draw Mens Souls into Perdition,
And when most needed, take them to their wings.

Ah foolish Man! that sets his heart upon   25
Such empty Shadows, such wild Fowl as these,
That being gotten will be quickly gone.
And whilst they stay increase but his disease

As in a Dropsie, drinking draughts begets,
The more he drinks, the more he still requires: 30
So on this world whoso affection sets,
His Wealths encrease encreaseth his desires.

O happy Man, whose portion is above,
Where Floods, where Flames, where Foes cannot bereave him;
Most wretched man, that fixed hath his love   35
Upon this World, that surely will deceive him!

For, what is *Honour*? What is *Sov'raignty*,
Whereto mens hearts so restlesly aspire?
Whom have they Crowned with Felicity?
When did they ever satisfie desire?   40

The Ear of Man with hearing is not fill'd:
To see new sights still coveteth the Eye:
The craving Stomack though it may be still'd,
Yet craves again without a new supply.

All Earthly things, man's Cravings answer not,   45
Whose little heart would all the World contain,
(If all the World should fall to one man's Lot)
And notwithstanding empty still remain,

The Eastern Conquerour was said to weep,
When he the Indian Ocean did view,   50
To see his Conquest bounded by the Deep,
And no more Worlds remaining to subdue.

Who would that man in his Enjoyments bless,
Or envy him, or covet his estate,
Whose gettings do augment his greediness,   55
And make his wishes more intemperate?

Such is the wonted and the common guise
Of those on Earth that bear the greatest Sway:
If with a few the case be otherwise
They seek a Kingdom that abides for ay.   60

Moreover they, of all the Sons of men,
that Rule, and are in Highest Places set,
Are most inclin'd to scorn their Bretheren
And God himself (without great grace) forget.

For as the Sun doth blind the gazer's eyes,   65
That for a time they nought discern aright:
So Honour doth befool and blind the Wise,
And their own Lustre 'reaves them of their sight.

Great are their Dangers, manifold their Cares;
Thro which, whilst others Sleep, they scarcely Nap;   70
And yet are oft surprised unawares,
And fall unweeting into Envies Trap.

The mean Mechanick finds his kindly rest
All void of fear Sleepeth the Country-Clown:
When greatest Princes often are distrest,   75
And cannot Sleep upon their Beds of Down.

Could *Strength* or *Valour* men Immortalize,
Could *Wealth* or *Honour* keep them from decay,
There were some cause the same to Idolize,
And give the lye to that which I do say.   80

But neither can such things themselves endure
Without the hazard of a Change one hour,
Nor such as trust in them can they secure
From dismal dayes, or Deaths prevailing pow'r.

If *Beauty* could the beautiful defend   85
From Death's dominion, than fair *Absalom*
Had not been brought to such a shameful end:
But fair and foul into the Grave must come.

If *Wealth* or *Scepters* could Immortal make,
Then wealthy *Croesus*, wherefore art thou dead?   90
If *Warlike force*, which makes the World to quake,
Then why is *Julius Caesar* perished?

Where are the *Scipio's* Thunder-bolts of War?
Renowned *Pompey*, *Caesars* Enemie?
Stout *Hannibal*, *Romes* Terror known so far?   95
Great *Alexander*, what's become of thee?

If *Gifts* and *Bribes* Death's favour might but win,
If *Power*, if force, or *Threatnings* might it fray,
All these, and more, had still surviving been:
But all are gone, for Death will have no Nay.   100

Such is this World with all her Pomp and Glory,
Such are the men whom worldly eyes admire:
Cut down by Time, and now become a Story,
That we might after better things aspire.

Go boast thy self of what thy heart enjoyes,   105
Vain Man! triumph in all thy worldly Bliss:
Thy best enjoyments are but Trash and Toyes:
Delight thy self in that which worthless is.

Omnia praetereunt praeter amare Deum.

BOSTON PUBLIC LIBRARY

3 9999 03618 257 2

Other titles from American Eagle Publications include:

The Captive, by Mary Rowlandson, is the famous narrative of her life among the Indians after her capture in 1676 during King Phillip's War in New England.

The Hawks of Hawk Hollow, by Robert Montgomery Bird, an exciting novel about the revolution, originally published in 1835.

The Plays of Robert Munford, *The Candidates* and *The Patriots*. The Oldest Comic Plays Written in America, dating back to the 1780's.

The Little Black Book of Computer Viruses, a fascinating exposé of how computer viruses work, including source code for four different viruses.

For a free descriptive catalog, write to:

American Eagle Publications, Inc.
Post Office Box 41401-K
Tucson, Arizona 85717